DIS

CW00552659

"This is an important and illu:
two persistent and intractabl

levels of population health and the injustice of inequalities in
health. Read this book and feel your outrage, then read it again to
focus on what we need to do to create transformative change."

KATE PICKETT, Professor of Epidemiology,
University of York, and co-author of *The Spirit Level*

"This conceptually and empirically rich book outlines how health
and disease have been unequally experienced across the country both
before and during the Covid-19 pandemic. It argues powerfully that we
cannot go back to 'business as usual' and should instead harness a new
'spirit of '45' to truly build back better and reduce health inequalities."

CLARE BAMBRA, Professor of Public Health,
Newcastle University

"Fran Pollock sets out the hard truth of how political choices
have deprioritized ordinary people's health and well-being and
sets out how we can stand together to oblige leaders to protect
us all. Reading her book shocks but also empowers us to act."

BEN PHILLIPS, author of *How to Fight Inequality*

FIVE GIANTS: A NEW BEVERIDGE REPORT

Consultant editor: Danny Dorling, *University of Oxford*

In November 1942, William Beveridge published *Social Insurance and Allied Services*, the result of a survey work commissioned the year before by the wartime coalition government. In what soon became known as simply "The Beveridge Report", five impediments to social progress were identified: the giants of Want, Disease, Squalor, Ignorance and Idleness. Tackling these giants was to be at the heart of postwar reconstruction. The welfare state, including national insurance, child allowances and the National Health Service, was a direct result of Beveridge's recommendations.

To mark the eightieth anniversary of the Report's publication, the authors in this series consider the progress made against Beveridge's giants, and whether they have diminished or risen up to again stalk the land. They also reflect on how the fight against poverty, unfit housing, ill-health, unemployment and poor education could be renewed as the countries of the UK emerge from a series of deeply damaging, divisive and impoverishing crises.

As an establishment figure, a Liberal and a eugenicist, Beveridge was an unlikely coordinator of the radical changes that improved so many peoples' lives. However, the banking crisis at the end of the 1920s, the mass unemployment and impoverishment of the 1930s, and the economic shock of the Second World War changed what was possible to what became essential. Old certainties were swept aside as much from within the existing order as from outside it.

The books explore the topic without constraint and the results are informative, entertaining and concerning. They aim to ignite a broader debate about the future of our society and encourage the vision and aspiration that previous generations held for us.

Want by Helen Barnard

Disease by Frances Darlington-Pollock

Squalor by Daniel Renwick and Robbie Shilliam

Ignorance by Sally Tomlinson

Idleness by Katy Jones and Ashwin Kumar

DISEASE

Frances Darlington-Pollock

agenda
publishing

In memory of Jonathan
For whom people meant more than politics.
Deeply loved and deeply missed.

© Frances Darlington-Pollock 2022

First published in 2022 by Agenda Publishing

Agenda Publishing Limited
The Core
Bath Lane
Newcastle Helix
Newcastle upon Tyne
NE4 5TF

www.agendapub.com

ISBN 978-1-78821-391-2
ISBN 978-1-78821-392-9 (ePDF)
ISBN 978-1-78821-393-6 (ePUB)

British Library Cataloguing-in-Publication Data
A catalogue record for this book is available
from the British Library

Typeset in Nocturne by Patty Rennie

Printed and bound in the UK by CPI Group (UK) Ltd,
Croydon, CR0 4YY

Contents

Acknowledgements

Many of the debates and underpinning ideas within this book are things I have been thinking on for a long time. Over the years, colleagues and friends have played a role in shaping, challenging and furthering those arguments and I thank them for that. But there are some people who have played a more formative role in this book, and they deserve particular mention. First and foremost, my editor Alison Howson. She understood my vision and gave me direction and constructive critique when needed. Danny Dorling for the opportunity and review. Herb for the discussion and comments on earlier drafts. And finally, thank you to Deborah, Paul, Claire and Alex for their encouragement and support.

The views presented in this book are my own, and do not necessarily represent those of my employers or affiliated organizations.

Frances Darlington-Pollock

1

Introduction: a revolutionary moment

A revolutionary moment in the world's history is a time for revolution, not for patching.

Beveridge, *Social Insurance and Allied Services*

In 1969, Johan Galtung introduced the concept of "structural violence". He urged that we consider how and in what ways violence could be construed as more than the physical act of harm from one body to another, and how the very society we inhabit acts to prevent people from realizing their full potential. In establishing this expanded concept of violence, Galtung offered a definition which is strikingly resonant today: "if a person died from tuberculosis in the eighteenth century it would be hard to conceive of this as violence since it might have been quite unavoidable, but if he dies from it today, despite all the medical resources in the world, then violence is present" (Galtung 1969: 168). What of today? December 2019 saw the emergence of a new, highly infectious disease targeting the lungs and other organs to devastating effect. Alarm grew in the scientific and medical community as to both its severity and transmissibility, with the rise of outbreaks in care homes and hospitals flagged to the UK government as early as January 2020 (Blanchard 2020). This failed to translate into political action. Two years into the pandemic and more than 150,000 people had died from Covid-19 in the UK alone. Many of these deaths were avoidable.

Ignoring warnings from officially appointed scientific experts, in the early days of the pandemic the UK government chose not to mandate testing older people for Covid-19 when discharged from hospital back into residential care. The consequences were severe: 40 per cent of the 48,213 people who died from Covid-19 in the first wave (mid-March to mid-June 2020) were care home residents (Scobie 2021). As late as 3 March 2020, Prime Minister Boris Johnson was boasting about shaking hands with "everybody" in a Covid-19-infected hospital (Weaver 2020). But as the pandemic unfolded, the rising rates of infection and mounting death toll forced action. Escalating messages to "shield", avoid public transport and practice good hygiene and social distancing gave way to national lockdowns. However, preventative measures to halt the spread of the deadly virus all favoured the more privileged segments of society. A new hierarchy of employment emerged, with those occupations deemed as essential operating at the coalface of the pandemic and bearing the brunt of the risk. Desperate attempts to ensure compliance with the much-needed public health measures introduced saw political messaging appeal to the public's love of the National Health Service (NHS): "Stay home, protect the NHS, save lives". At the same time, the prime minister and his early blasé attitude to public health advice remained apparent throughout much of the pandemic. Regular maskless media appearances paled into insignificance, however, amid the scandal of his and his inner-staff's extensive socializing in the depths of social-distancing rules. It was one rule for them and another for us.

The structural violence exposed by Covid-19 is impossible to ignore, wrought through the vulnerabilities of a diminished and diminishing welfare state, the policies that deny those most in need and the political rhetoric which in turn demonizes those already suffering. But emergent in that crisis were signs of a political attempt at renewal, reminiscent of the aims of the Committee on Reconstruction Problems set up some 80 years before. In November 1942, Sir William Beveridge presented this committee with a radical blueprint for what rapidly became one of the most admired manifestations of the welfare state around the world. Rather than the devastation of a pandemic, this committee was tasked with charting a path out of the instability of a collapsing empire and the ravages of two successive world wars. Targeting "five giants" that stood between a flourishing society and the "road to reconstruction" in the aftermath of war – Want, Disease, Ignorance, Squalor and Idleness – Beveridge's report called for a revolutionary approach: a system of social security built on the principle of meaningful cooperation between the state and the individual. It was truly revolutionary, levying bipartisan support to rebuild a better Britain, supporting the population from cradle to grave. But as the decades passed, the reputation of something once so admired has seriously diminished. The Covid-19 pandemic's destructive, uneven sweep through the population exposed deep chasms in the manner of welfare provision in the UK, exacerbating the suffering of many still reeling from a decade of government austerity. We have access to some of the best medical resources in the world. The scale and extent of death and illness facing the UK's population today is, in fact, quite avoidable. Violence is present, and we again find ourselves in need of a revolution.

A TIME FOR REVOLUTION?

By the end of the Second World War, Britain had lost 384,000 soldiers in combat and the civilian death toll had reached 70,000. The global dominance of the British economy, shored up by a far-reaching empire, had begun to decline in the advent of deindustrialization. The threat of a disillusioned populace wondering what on earth they had fought and died for underpinned government concern over the future of Britain, its economy and its international dominance. How to prosper, to rebuild, to recover? Chairing an interdepartmental committee of representatives including the Home Office, Health, Labour and National Service, Pensions and Actuaries, Beveridge developed a radical position. He reported a robust critique of existing policies and schemes varyingly and discretely concerned with specific aspects of the welfare of the population. Beveridge damned the "piecemeal" approach inherent to prior reforms, such as the widely criticized but long-established Poor Laws of the nineteenth century, Compulsory Health Insurance (1912), Unemployment Insurance (1912) and the Pension Acts (1908, 1934), arguing for recognition of the interrelationships between these "allied problems". To achieve "freedom from want", Beveridge proposed a system of social insurance that both protected "against interruption and destruction of earning power and for special expenditure arising at birth, marriage or death" (Beveridge 1942: 9). Under this system, the population would be able to access a range of benefits related to unemployment, disability, training and maternity when needed, and could expect to be supported in retirement through pension provision. It went further still, establishing the NHS, with care provided free at the point of delivery: the first universal medical care system in the world. This was a landmark institution heralding a raft of improvements to individual and population health and one that, for many, is the focus of an enduring admiration of the British welfare state.

When Beveridge submitted his report in November 1942, life expectancy at birth was around 66 for women and 60 for men. And, for every 1,000 live births there were 52.9 deaths in the first 12 months of life. But fertility rates were low. Beveridge – and many others – feared significant population decline. Although women had gained status during the war years, filling labour shortages as men fought, in the aftermath of war societal expectations of women did not extend much further than the hearth or the nursery. Beveridge clearly captured this sentiment in his design of benefits entitlement, producing a decidedly pro-marital, pro-natal set of policies he thought necessary to reverse the falling fertility rates of the 1930s. Unbeknown to Beveridge at the time of writing, fertility had actually been increasing and would soon climb above the number of live births per woman needed to maintain the population. Indeed, this was the advent of the generation known as the baby boomers and signalled a significant change in the size and structure of the population. It was certainly a time of revolution.

But what ensured this radical vision for our welfare state's success? It was not just political unease that drove the adoption of such a radical shift of responsibility for the welfare of the population from people to state. Reaching sales of more than half a million within two months of publication, the public devoured Beveridge's vision. The population was struggling before the onset of war. The collapse of Wall Street in October 1929 sent shock waves around the world, decimating global trade and, in the UK, pushing large swathes of the population into poverty and precarity. Although the working classes of the industrial north felt the Great Depression keenly, the middle classes were not unscathed. In the safety net afforded by Beveridge's blueprint for a welfare state were signs of a response to their demands for action and support. It is difficult not to draw parallels with today. The trauma of Covid-19 speaks, for some, to the trauma of war. Although we would be naïve to think that a "Blitz spirit" united us all in the experience of such an unequal pandemic, the increasing precarity experienced by some of the middle classes is indeed reminiscent of their experiences through the Great Depression and the subsequent chaos of war.

BUILDING A WELFARE STATE

At the heart of Beveridge's vision was a system of compulsory insurance granting access to the full breadth of benefits available for all those insured. Taken as a single contribution from weekly or monthly pay packets, all workers contributed to the national pot, protecting not only them and their families from cradle to grave but also the injured or sick who were unable to work, the widowed and children without parents. Based on the premise that a working nation was a healthy, prosperous nation, the plan aspired to full employment, with all contributing to resource universal access to the education and healthcare that the goals of full employment and prosperity in turn depended on. The family was the focal point for Beveridge's system of provision and payment: a male worker supported by a female carer who eschewed paid work for the greater task of raising a family, and by extension a nation (1942: 49). This system of contribution for the entirety of one's working life meant that the national contributions' pot, under Beveridge's assumption of full employment, would always be sustained through a favourable balance between the working, contributing man and the smaller proportion of dependents, whether children, wives (although Beveridge considered wives as partners rather than dependents), retirees or those temporarily unable to work.

Although Beveridge's proposals were, by any measure, radical, they were a reflection of the patriarchal system in which he lived. In considering not only what he proposed, but also, to some extent, what unfolded, we might raise the spectres of ableism, sexism and also racism. Under the proposals, ill-health was considered to be a deviant, temporary state that the wider system of insurance could readily resolve. Having taken advantage of universal healthcare after falling ill, the male breadwinner would resume working *and contributing*, having done so since they began employment and continuing to do so until they reached old age and retirement. Although women could also take advantage of universal healthcare, they were otherwise entirely dependent on their spouse for support once married (the expectation was that all would indeed marry). Women were then to meet all the care needs of their family not otherwise provided for by the state. But can all ill-health be treated? Are all women so ready to marry in lieu of work, and how much care work is then placed on their shoulders?

And what of the challenge of racism? Beveridge charged women with the lofty task of raising a nation, highlighting their "vital work . . . in ensuring the adequate continuance of the *British race* and of *British ideals*" (1942: 53, emphasis added). The ideals of a British "race" speaks to an assumption of superiority pulled from the dying flames of the British Empire. But the undercurrent of racism goes further than promoting racial superiority. It is tethered to the assumption that entitlement to welfare provision depended on compulsory contributions into the national pot for the entirety of one's working life. White, working men held that entitlement. Not women, not migrants, not even those migrants arriving in the *Windrush* years and after. Indeed, the welfare state that emerged post-Beveridge protected the white poor, institutionalizing their advantage over Black, Brown or other minoritized ethnic groups (Shilliam 2018).

Regardless of some of the language and ethos of Beveridge's report, its aspiration to build a healthy and therefore prosperous nation were still remarkable. The initial pay-offs of this system were significant, capitalizing on the sense of collective participation and shared interests across society at large prompted by the aftermath of war. Life expectancy increased as people began to reap the rewards of a universal, comprehensive healthcare service. The chances of surviving past the first days, months and years of life increased, and the rapidly expanding medical advances were, through the NHS, increasingly available to all. The population enjoyed better conditions of work and indeed unemployment, benefits entitlement grew, education expanded and the quality of and access to affordable homes improved. But we became complacent. We took these gains for granted and assumed they would continue without our continued investment.

DISMANTLING THE WELFARE STATE

The nature of welfare provision proposed by Beveridge was a clear departure from the status quo. The financial and physical well-being of the population were to be a matter for the state, facilitated by the willing financial contributions of its population. But although welfare was no longer a charitable gift to the poor, the language of Beveridge's vision is expressed in assumptions of the shortcomings of individuals. To live in squalor. To be idle. To be ignorant. To want. Although this is considered through the lens of modern values and linguistic conventions, it foreshadows the increasing transfer of responsibility for welfare from the state back to the individual and the realms of voluntary action. Beveridge wanted a flourishing, prosperous, stable nation, and one that was competitive in a capitalist global economy. By any accounts, this is what he delivered as subsequent governments enacted his vision – although in their own style. But over time, the solidarity and system of reciprocity so necessary to Beveridge's efforts to ensure a productive, prosperous nation have been eroded by the vagaries of a neoliberal capitalist society.

Couched in the liberal ideology that has since seen capitalist, neoliberal principles entrench, Beveridge's report regarded the health and well-being of the population as a means to an end rather than a goal in and of itself. A healthy, flourishing people were an economically prosperous nation. A healthy, flourishing people was to be an increasing population. As neoliberal political ideology matured in the UK, policy and political rhetoric became increasingly centred on the individual. At the same time, the market was given ever more primacy in economic debate in which competition principles are elevated as the key mechanisms through which to organize society, allocate resources and measure success. The role of the market and the individual created the space in which responsibility for health and well-being was gradually and progressively transferred from the state to the individual. Prioritizing the global competitiveness of the economy and the labour market came at the expense of a strong safety net of social protection, regulated wages and progressive taxation. The outcome has been a loss of the shared interests in maintaining a welfare state in which those who depend on it are increasingly demonized and marginalized by political rhetoric. And yet, the ideology which enables this demonization and emphasis on individual responsibility is the root cause of the growing numbers of people in urgent need of welfare support.

Beveridge was concerned with the fact of our poor health. But today, it is not simply the fact of poor health which challenges the welfare state. Nor is it just that although we live longer, many of us do so in poorer health. Our giant of disease is a discriminating monstrous beast stealing years of life expectancy simply because of who we are and where we live. Neither the existence of a universal, comprehensive healthcare service, nor the advances signalled by a combined attack on want, squalor, idleness and ignorance, have been enough to stop inequalities in health, well-being and longevity growing in society. Beveridge's welfare state has taken us as far as it can, compounded by the simple fact that the population Beveridge sought to support and see prosper no longer exists. It is no longer enough to weave a safety net just strong enough to hold people out of destitution. In fact, the net is now so full of holes that people literally fall through.

Structural violence is present when violence is "built into the structure [of society] and shows up as unequal power and consequently as unequal life chances" (Galtung 1969: 171). It is present in polarized, uneven income distributions. It manifests in the uneven distribution of resources and services. Most importantly, it is present and wrought through the uneven distribution of influence and of power. Who decides what resources are distributed where? Are income and wealth redistributed through tax? Is the provision of education and affordable housing equitable? Are all able to access gainful, secure employment? We live in violence, yet we are quite easily persuaded of its absence. A difference of as little as 20 miles to where you are born can return as much as a decade of additional life expectancy. This should not be possible in a welfare state that safeguards against want so that all can flourish and all can prosper. Disease alone is no longer the problem. It is the uneven structures through which we are either protected from or vulnerable to this giant's long reach.

STEMMING THE VIOLENCE?

Today, the composition, size and health profile of the population is dramatically different from 1942. And now, as in 1942, our provision of welfare needs more than patchy reform. The successes yielded by Beveridge's radical vision have taken us as far as they can. The NHS in its current form is no longer sustainable and unable to meet the demands of an older, larger, more ethnically diverse and sicker population. The narrowing of income inequality which emerged as the nation pulled together in the aftermath of war has reversed, and in recent years we have seen an unprecedented period of loss in real earnings. Austerity's squeeze on budgets and significant economic inequality is the context within which life expectancy, despite major improvements since Beveridge's day, have stalled at a rate not seen since the late 1800s. It is the backdrop against which we live longer but often in poorer health. It is the environment where significant improvements in health outcomes and healthcare are countered by rises in long-term conditions such as diabetes, expanding waistlines and deteriorating mental health. It is the circumstances under which a global pandemic can become endemic in deprived, marginalized communities, with politicians shifting responsibility for the spread of disease to vulnerable populations.

Beveridge sought to create a system that, if successful, would "make want under any circumstances unnecessary" (1942: 9). By implication, he surely hoped to conquer ignorance, squalor, idleness and of course disease. Yet are all conquerable? Others in this series will evaluate the extent to which we have and can make want unnecessary, fight ignorance, banish squalor and challenge idleness. But in these pages we consider the evolving giant of Disease, itself impossible to separate from the inequities, the inequalities and the disadvantages that characterize the remaining four giants. And what of that evolving giant? In tracing the evolution of disease since Beveridge's day, we see an expanded idea of health, an expanded health *and social* care system and therefore space for new interventions in tackling the modern-day giants stalking our health and well-being.

2

Disease: an evolving giant

Hælth – From WHOLE, a being whole, sound, or well.

The first duty of Beveridge's committee was to survey existing national schemes of social insurance and allied services; the second was to make recommendations. Such a survey cannot have been an easy undertaking, but can you imagine conducting a similar one today? Consider, for example, the sheer complexity of welfare provision exposed through the chaos of universal credit introduced in 2013. Somehow, in seeking to simplify benefit payments and streamline six separate schemes into one, the system became even more complex. Or imagine trying to unpack exactly why, during a global health crisis, one set of benefit recipients would be deemed in need of a temporary uplift to their payments while others would not. And that is just those services that, supposedly, safeguard against want. But what would a survey of the services and schemes of today actually conclude? What would Beveridge recommend now? It is tempting, in a discussion such as this, to reel off the latest questionable decisions on service provision; or perhaps to spend time dissecting decisions that seem to have been motivated by short-term budgetary constraints rather than long-term planning. A biography of such changes to welfare and service provision is not, however, our task in this book.

Instead, we are surveying progress in tackling Beveridge's giant of Disease given the foundations he laid for our welfare state, and making recommendations to tackle that giant, which is somehow more monstrous today. To begin, we need a picture of the contemporary giant of Disease, tracing its evolution from the infections, emerging chronic diseases and relatively short lifespans of 1942 to the behemoth of today.

MORE THAN THE ABSENCE OF DISEASE

In general, how would you rate your health? In the UK, this may sound a familiar question, at least to anyone who has completed the decennial census. In the census, you are encouraged to consider any aspect of your health that you think is relevant. So, what is relevant? The criteria you use to evaluate your health in the last year might be different from that which you would have used five years ago, or as a child, or as you might in the final stages of your life. But the criteria you probably use to evaluate your own health doesn't just change as you age, it will also change depending on when you are aging. Would a child growing up in eighteenth-century Britain, be they in the slums of an industrial town or the riches of a country estate, have made the same sorts of assessment of their health as you will have made as a child?

The points of reference we use to benchmark our own health vary depending on the social, economic, political and historic contexts in which we are born, age and die. In times of severe hardship, as indeed eighteenth-century life in Britain was for many, simply being alive, and able to get up and go to work, may have been enough to yield a relatively positive assessment of one's health. But today, were you in an equivalent state of hardship, would you still be able to offer such a positive assessment? It is likely that, when evaluating your health as you read this, you have reflected on whether or not you have a chronic disease or an acute infection. But you probably also considered the conditions in which you live, your sense of security and the sorts of things to which you have access to maintain your well-being. Health is more than the absence of disease.

The World Health Organization's (WHO) definition of "health" is reflective of that: "a state of *complete* physical, mental and social well-being and not merely the absence of disease or infirmity" (1948, emphasis added). Enshrined in its Constitution of 1948, this definition is perhaps more aspirational than factual for many around the world. Nevertheless, it harks back to the Germanic origins of the world "health", related to the word "whole" or "a being whole, sound, or well" (*Chambers Dictionary of Etymology* 2008: 470). Such an all-encompassing definition is important as it created the conceptual space for a move away from traditional biomedical approaches to understanding and treating (ill-) health. Biomedical approaches prioritize diagnosing and treating the biologically deviant state of disease (*dis-ease*) at the expense of other, less tangible, ailments or concerns over the wider contexts that shape health for individuals and populations. Biomedical models are limited to the physical, material state of the body, whereas social models as implied by the WHO definition of health embrace a more expansive concept. These take seriously the ways in which individual experiences of well-being, illness and disability, associated with different physical, material states of the body, are influenced by social factors. Health and illness become relative concepts: socially constructed phenomena amenable to the social, economic, political and historic contexts in which we live.

Despite the relative novelty of alternative approaches to biomedical understandings of health, attention to wider environmental conditions beyond the immediate control of the individual actually have a long and esteemed history. Hippocrates, the Greek physician often touted as the father of medicine, penned the book *On Airs, Waters and Places* around 400 BCE. The book opens with an explicit direction to look to climate and weather, and to differences in locations and situation, as well as to the behaviours of different people in different places for "whoever wishes to investigate medicine properly". Although this attention to those conditions beyond the immediate control of the individual did lessen in the intervening centuries, the "great sanitary awakening" in Victorian Britain saw a renewed interest (Wilmslow 1923). Sir Edwin Chadwick, in 1842, famously reported on the sanitary conditions of the working classes, linking poor living conditions to differences in both the rates and severity of disease and life expectancy. Poor health and illness were no longer simply understood as the inevitable consequences of corrupt morals but in some way related to the wider social context and environment. Responsibility for poor health became a matter of public concern rather than just a failing of an individual. Advances in germ theory and the growing ability to vaccinate against infectious diseases marked a shift in how this particular branch of medicine – public health – approached maintaining good health in the population. Although assumptions as to where responsibility for either poor or good health rests now are contested (as we shall see), sensibility to the importance of the wider environment has not been lost. Today, the shift in how health, and therefore illness, disease and disability, is understood and represented in society occurred at the same time as a reordering of the leading causes of death in the Western world. Concurrently, the morbidity profile of the population – the nature of what ails us – has also changed. As societies develop, so too it appears do the things that kill us and the conditions that make us ill. Frequent epidemics, natural disasters, endemic diseases and intractable famine once blighted populations. And, notwithstanding the dual threat of Covid-19 and climate change, those savage conditions and the toll of infectious diseases had gradually loosened their grip, to be replaced by more amenable conditions and delayed, degenerative and lifestyle diseases. Attention to how we understand and represent health is important for our discussion of Beveridge's giant of Disease.

It not only serves as a marker for progress but also acts as the framework upon which we can build a new call for radical action.

RECEDING PANDEMICS
AND DEGENERATIVE DISEASE

Some 50 years ago, Abdel R. Omran (1971) articulated a series of transitions in the mortality profile of populations, setting these changes in the context of wider transitions in the demographic, sociologic and economic situation of different societies. Known as the "epidemiologic transition", this theory looks to the leading causes of death and how they change as societies modernize: life expectancy increases as the leading causes of death shift from infectious diseases towards chronic, non-communicable disease. Concurrently, the growth trajectories and structure of populations – their distribution by age and sex – will also change. Omran defined three phases of transition, moving from the age of pestilence and famine, to receding pandemics, before ending with degenerative lifestyle diseases (for example, Type 2 diabetes, heart disease or strokes). Originally formulated as a means to both describe and explain the shifting mortality profile of populations (i.e. the changes in the leading causes of death), Omran placed considerable emphasis on modernization over advances in medicine and public health in driving those changes, an emphasis that remains controversial. No small part of the debate stems from wider evidence of the "critical challenges and threats" that economic development can pose to population health and welfare (Szreter 1997). Nevertheless, Omran's theory still offers a useful framework in which to consider how the health of the British population has changed since Beveridge's day. Subsequent revisions to Omran's original proposition illuminate some of the health challenges faced by an ageing population – the extent of which Beveridge could not have anticipated – and the emerging threats to contemporary society. But first, to better understand the context in which Beveridge was writing, we need to look back across the preceding century and trace the British transition from the age of receding pandemics to that of degenerative disease.

The slums of the industrial revolution were hotbeds for disease, with cities vividly described as "graveyards" and "demographic sinks" (Woods 2003: 30). The poor living conditions characterized by overcrowded households and cities, poor-quality accommodation, dirty streets and poor sanitation saw smallpox, cholera and tuberculosis flourish. Children faced a particularly high risk, and of those who did survive as many as one in five would die before their fifteenth birthday. Yet not all suffered equally. Sir Edwin Chadwick's investigation into the sanitary conditions of Britain's working population, published a hundred years before Beveridge's report, produced a now famed table comparing the average age of death between Rutland, Liverpool, Bolton, Leeds and Manchester. Yet it wasn't just about where you lived (and died), it also seemed to matter who you were, at least in terms of your occupation. The labourers of Rutland died, on average, aged 38. This was some years earlier than either the local tradesman (41) or professionals (52). But should that labourer, tradesman or professional happen to live and work in Bolton, they would probably not see past their 18th, 23rd, or 34th birthday, respectively. But progress was made. We saw rapid improvements in life expectancy, particularly over the last century, built on the medical advances and developments in public health pursued in the late nineteenth and early twentieth century. For example, although premised on the erroneous belief that miasmas (bad airs) were a source of disease, better sanitation in hospitals and cities (i.e. the Sanitary Movement), alongside the eventual yet begrudging acceptance that washing hands before treating patients was sensible, reduced the threat and impact of infectious disease. Later, compulsory vaccinations emerging through advances in germ theory also contributed to progress in eradicating different infectious diseases and thereby raising life expectancy.

By the turn of the twentieth century, the divisions once reported by Chadwick – and the sense of public responsibility for population health that it had once heralded – again became a matter of prominent political and public concern. This was particularly true among the healthier middle classes when faced with the poor health of working-class foot soldiers. Increasing concern for the health of the nation and its soldiers in the face of war were the very foundations needed to drive through a more universal system of health coverage than had previously existed. This coincided with continued and significant changes in the health profile of the population. But setting aside the military and civilian costs of war, the leading causes of death in the 1940s were still rather different from those faced by people today. Although 4,700 children died in the air raids of 1940 and 1941, 7,878 more died from infectious diseases such as tuberculosis, pneumonia and diphtheria. Such high numbers of deaths translate into a very high infant mortality rate: for every 1,000 live births there were 5.29 deaths in the first 12 months of life. Wartime had reintroduced some of the overcrowding and intermingling of the population reminiscent of the industrial revolution, reawakening some of its infectious diseases in spite of the wider receding of associated pandemics and Britain's alleged entry into the age of degenerative diseases. Respiratory conditions such as tuberculosis and bronchopneumonia were among the major drivers of mortality across men and women, particularly in younger age groups. Yet the toll of infectious disease did continue to rescind, responding both to the ongoing developments in public health and medical care and to wider improvements in the social and economic conditions of the population. Notably, for example, deaths from diseases such as tuberculosis, diphtheria, measles and whooping cough were all but nonexistent in children by the 1960s.

As infectious diseases began to loosen their grip, other drivers of mortality took hold. For children, first most notably among boys aged between five and 14, motor vehicle accidents emerged as the leading cause of death in the early 1940s and remained a significant threat until the mid-1980s and the introduction of compulsory seatbelts. But more striking was the emergence of non-communicable diseases and their now continued role in shaping the mortality profile and age structure of the population. Omran had in fact pointed to the marked increase in cardio-vascular deaths in Britain since 1945 in his seminal paper. This was particularly apparent for men aged 35 and over, whereas for women cancers were among the most common causes of death. Where the leading causes of death in a population shift from infectious to non-communicable diseases, the age structure of the population shifts upwards. Children and young adults are particularly vulnerable to infectious disease. As they survive into middle and older ages, their risk of death from degenerative disease increases. Just as Beveridge failed to anticipate how progress in the very welfare state he sought to create would lead to continued improvements in life expectancy – and new challenges of morbidity – so Omran's theory failed to capture how the rates of improvements to life expectancy would continue in his so-called "modernized" societies. Nor did it capture the degree to which continued medical advances would sustain older generations and thereby delay the fatality of manmade, degenerative diseases. A fourth stage was thus added to Omran's theory: the age of *delayed* degenerative diseases in which the mortality from non-communicable diseases shifts into advanced ages (people aged 80 and above) (Olshanksy & Ault 1986). Omran and others were writing at a time when confidence in the eradication of different infectious diseases did not feel misplaced. But although the global toll of non-communicable diseases is significant, we now know with the certainty of lived experience that Albert Camus was right in his assertion that "pestilences have a way of recurring in the world". Indeed, Mark Honigsbaum's (2020) overview of a century of pandemics, from the Spanish flu of 1918 right up to Covid-19 of 2020, unequivocally demonstrates this. What

kills and ails us may well have changed in the years since Beveridge dreamed of "a national health service for prevention and for
cure of disease and disability by medical treatment" (1942: 158).
But just how much?

BECOMING A BEHEMOTH

In 1942, life expectancy at birth was around 66 years for women
and 60 for men. At the turn of the twenty-first century, women
had gained nearly 14 years whereas men gained closer to 15.
Deaths in younger age groups and the prevalence of infectious
disease in a population has a sizeable impact on overall life expectancy. Such gains are not then unexpected given the sensitivity
of either deaths in younger ages or the prevalence of infectious
diseases to wider environmental factors. This includes the level
of overcrowding in households and cities, or the degree of sanitation. Improved living conditions, better lifestyles and the medical
advances of the postwar period were the engine accelerating what
has since manifested as a century-long period of sustained annual
improvements in life expectancy. The scale of this improvement
is clear to see in Figure 2.1, plotting life expectancy at birth for the
population of England and Wales by sex between 1841 and 2020.
In the UK more widely, by 2019 and just before the global pandemic of Covid-19 hit, life expectancy at birth had reached 83.1
for women and 79.4 for men. The gains in life expectancy at birth
mirrored improvements in infant mortality rates in the population (see Chapter 4), falling from the 52.9 per 1,000 live births of
Beveridge's day to around 3.5 in 2019.

However, we reached the tail end of that period of sustained
improvements for life expectancy around 2014. From 2014, the
rate of improvement begins to falter. At the same time, infant
mortality rates also begin to increase. For England and Wales,
this followed a record low of 3.6 deaths per 1,000 live births. Life
expectancy may well be the ultimate marker of health, but any

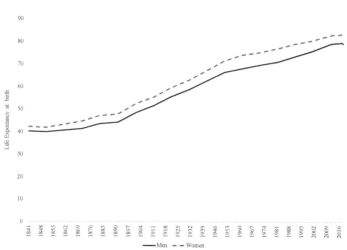

Figure 2.1   Life expectancy at birth, England and Wales,
1841–2020.

Source: Office for National Statistics (2015, 2020a) (based on historic and
contemporary national life tables).

increase in infant mortality is the waning canary in the coalmine:
an early warning of deteriorating health in a population and, as
we will see in Chapter 4, undeniable evidence of the deadly consequences of inequality and structural violence in our society.
Coincident with the faltering life expectancy of 2014, and the
nudging upwards of infant mortality, we saw one of the largest
annual increases in mortality since the Second World War in
2015. People aged 70 and over bore the brunt of this increase, with
many subsequently arguing that the fiscal austerity introduced in
response to the global financial crisis of 2008 had much to answer
for, both in respect of the huge increase in deaths and the stalling
life expectancy. Even before Covid-19 surfaced, questions about
"excess mortality" and unequal chances of a long and healthy life
had begun to emerge. The onslaught of a global pandemic has simply intensified these debates. In 2020, for example, Public Health

England placed life expectancy in England at its lowest since 2011, falling to 82.7 for women and 78.7 for men (Public Health England 2021). We will return to these debates in more detail in Chapter 7. For now, although the recent picture of life expectancy in the UK and child mortality is one of faltering improvements and eroding gains, we have as a population seen marked and significant improvements since Beveridge's era.

However, the welfare state Beveridge imagined was for a very different population. It was one where people were not likely to live past their mid-sixties and were killed either by infectious respiratory conditions as children and young adults or by cancers and cardiovascular diseases *if* they reached middle or older age. Over time, the infectious diseases gradually featured less, and substance abuse, suicide and self-harm were among the leading causes of death for younger men and women. More recently, the perhaps inevitable consequence of surviving into middle, older and even advanced ages are the elevated risks of succumbing to degenerative diseases later in life. Indeed, dementias – those delayed degenerative diseases – increasingly characterize the mortality profile of the population, whereas cardiovascular deaths (heart conditions and strokes) have been decreasing. In 2018, dementia was the leading killer in the UK, accounting for 12.7 per cent of all deaths and becoming the leading cause of death for women (Office for National Statistics 2020b). Although part of this increasing prevalence is a consequence of us living longer, it is also the result of a national policy drive to increase formal diagnoses of dementia in England and changes to the way in which cause of death is coded on death certificates. It is worth highlighting, however, that should all forms of cancer be grouped together when reporting cause of death, just as all forms of dementia including Alzheimer's currently are, cancers would actually have accounted for 27 per cent of all deaths in 2018.

Although increased longevity in the population naturally elevates individual risk of death from degenerative diseases such as dementia, the nature of need and ill-health has also shifted dramatically across the entire age structure of the population. In some ways, this is to be celebrated. Consider, for example, the life expectancy of a child born with Down's syndrome in the 1940s compared to now: they were unlikely to live past their twelfth birthday, whereas today their life expectancy has climbed to 58. Or what of the chances of those diagnosed with the newly described "fibrocystic disease of the pancreas"? In the 1940s very little was known about the causes or consequences of this "chronic debilitation of infancy and early life" (Bean 1957: 321). While one study in the United States suggests that life expectancy cannot have been much more than 15 years (May 1944), elsewhere it is reported that children with this condition rarely lived past their fifth birthday. But today, of those born with what we now refer to as cystic fibrosis (a condition that can affect multiple organs such the pancreas and the lungs), half of those babies will survive into their thirties and beyond if the recent rates of improvement continue. The advent of a universal healthcare system, free at the point of use, imagined by Beveridge and implemented by Bevan, contributed to the improvements seen in the life chances of babies born with genetic disorders from 1940s onwards. In their chance of a life, their birth had new meaning for their loved ones. Rather than the pain and trauma of seeing your child's life curtailed, medical advances gave hope. The crisis of Covid-19 has, however, illuminated the shadows in which decisions of whose life has meaning and value, and indeed just how much value, are made. It is hard not to question why, when we applaud the medical advances that give hope of life to children and young adults who once may not have survived, we then seem to deem them as expendable at times of crisis. Nevertheless, the prohibitive costs of treating chronic long-term conditions, which had once heralded an early death, were no longer a barrier to the average working family. At the same time, improving living conditions and advances in medical and public health knowledge continued.

Although the increased rates of survival for people with chronic health conditions is nothing but a success, it does introduce new vulnerability in the population that again Beveridge could not have foreseen. Comorbidity – a tricky to define and contested concept, but for our purposes best understood simply as the simultaneous occurrence of two or more often overlapping conditions – has dramatically increased. First defined in 1970, the concept of comorbidity represents a direct response to the complexities of diagnosis and treatment in a population whose ill-health is increasingly defined by *multiple* chronic health conditions (Feinstein 1970). If you fall and break your leg while you have flu, you are suffering from more than one ailment. But the occurrence of the flu is not related to nor necessarily exacerbated by the fact of the broken leg. For a person living with dementia, however, hypertension (high blood pressure), coronary heart disease and diabetes may complicate their experience of dementia, whether in terms of treatment or outcomes. Key to the concept of comorbidity is that a primary condition, usually chronic, can be compromised and itself compromise co-occurring conditions. In the wider context of population ageing and delayed degenerative diseases, comorbidities of dementia, often undiagnosed, are particularly problematic. Beveridge's giant has become a behemoth.

Comorbid diseases extend beyond the physical, material state of the body – to reinvoke those shifting understandings and representations of health outlined earlier – to also capture the psychological and emotional well-being of the mind. Where once those suffering from mental health conditions were hidden away from society, sequestered in asylums and subjected to questionable at best, indefensible at worst, "therapy", the adoption of social models of health has coincided with a new level of awareness and acceptance of mental illness. There is of course considerable scope for improvement in how we, as a society, respond to and treat mental ill-health, particularly with respect to the stigma it carries. And although the increased awareness of mental illness will contribute to an increase in prevalence, this is only part of the picture. The behemoth of disease can then be seen not only in its increasing complexity but also in the changing mental health of the population. Turning first to clinically diagnosable conditions, depression and anxiety are common comorbid diseases, both of which have seen significant increases in recent years. Globally, more than 264 million people of all ages are thought to suffer from depression, to varying degrees of severity. In England, an analysis of adolescent mental health revealed increases in the frequency and severity of symptoms of anxiety and depression over a 20-year period (Collishaw *et al.* 2010). Professors Richard Wilkinson and Kate Pickett (2018) unpack some of the causes of our deteriorating mental health in high-income countries, pointing to the income inequality that is also consistently related to wider disadvantage in social, economic and other health outcomes. The burden of poor mental health, like so many health outcomes, is not, therefore, evenly distributed. Between 2013 and 2020 across England, for example, areas where more people were claiming universal credit also saw an increase in the use of antidepressants (Pybus *et al.* 2021). Deprivation isn't enough to explain this increase, although rates of universal credit claimants are higher in more deprived areas. The association between the proportion of people claiming universal credit in an area and increases in use of antidepressants is a damning illumination of the current failings of our welfare system.

Covid-19 did nothing to lessen the burden, exposing more and more people to precarity, grief and isolation in their day-to-day lives, which are important risk factors for poor mental health. In fact, estimates suggest that through the first 12 months of the pandemic, an additional 53.2 million cases of severe depression and a further 76.2 million cases of anxiety were reported globally. Universal credit claimants were particularly vulnerable, as Aurora, a widowed parent of two primary school-aged children from London, makes only too clear: "Our rent alone is over 95 percent of our total benefits ... Our situation is precarious, we struggle enormously and have done for many reasons. I feel like an utter failure" (Pybus *et al.* 2021: 6).

Beveridge set out to create a safety net to catch people before they hit rock bottom, to safeguard against want and to build towards a better future in the aftermath of war. Aurora is not a failure; the system failed and should have supported her. Our discussion of the prevalence of mental *ill*-health in the population does not, however, stop at clinically diagnosable conditions or disorder, as we can see from Aurora's experience. The WHO's definition of mental health is as expansive as its definition of "health" more generally. Where health is more than the absence of disease, so too is mental health more than the absence of mental disorders. It is, to quote the WHO, "an integral and essential component of health ... a state of well-being in which an individual realizes [their] own abilities, can cope with the normal stresses of life, can work productively and is able to make a contribution to [their] community" (World Health Organization 2018). Although perhaps not as lofty or aspirational a statement as the definition of health, it is similarly ambiguous. What are the normal stresses of life? And why should mental health be defined according to productivity at work (if we assume, as many typically do, that work equates with paid labour)? Nevertheless, attention to our well-being allows us to ask questions about general happiness, life satisfaction and the quality of our relationships, whether at home, in our local community or at work. Since April 2011, measures of personal well-being have been collected for England, Wales and Scotland, expanding to Northern Ireland a year later. These metrics report levels of life satisfaction at country, regional and local authority level, as well as whether respondents feel what they do in life is worthwhile, whether they felt happy yesterday and how anxious they felt yesterday. It is notable that, despite overall increases in clinical diagnoses of depression and anxiety, self-assessments of personal well-being paint a more positive picture, at least between 2011 and 2019. Levels of life satisfaction, feeling worthwhile and happiness were on the increase, whereas feeling anxious (rather than a clinical diagnosis of anxiety) were on the decrease. But the degree of change in well-being was not necessarily universal. For example, the greatest increases in average levels of happiness (measured as percentage change) were seen in North Warwickshire (+15.01), North West Leicestershire (+14.41) and Woking (+13.52). Yet 51 local areas saw a decline in happiness over the same period, with Surrey Heath (−7.32), South Northamptonshire (−5.03) and Daventry (−4.80) seeing the biggest declines.

THE BEHEMOTH'S FUTURE?

Mark Honigsbaum's (2020) revised edition of *The Pandemic Century*, ushered out with the advent of Covid-19, concludes with a reflection on our collective refusal to heed the warnings of virologists and others of the impending arrival of a catastrophically fatal virus. One can only hope, as deaths from Covid-19 are eventually tallied, that such ignorance is a thing of the past. The giant of Disease is indeed more monstrous than that which blocked the path to recovery for Beveridge's society. Our welfare state of today has much to contend with. The persistence of lifestyle and degenerative diseases, albeit some of which whose grip is amenable to medical intervention; the re-emergence of infectious diseases once thought defeated; and the emergence of new, novel viruses rapidly able to spread globally. Contemporary society also evidently takes its toll on our mental health, influencing well-being, life satisfaction and general happiness. The health system as currently structured is not capable of dealing with this behemoth, which is still modelled on the design Beveridge articulated. His attention to want, squalor, ignorance and idleness alongside the giant of disease foretold greater interest in the interdependence of those different domains of life as central to fostering human flourishing, health and well-being. But the drive for individualism, so dominant in society today, has eroded the sort of collective participation and responsibility that would ensure human flourishing and a shared interest in meaningfully safeguarding the health, security and prosperity of all. What, then, does it mean for health and well-being in a society where policy and public debate is too often couched in terms of self-interested individualism?

3

Unequal health and the behemoth of today

How long do you expect to live for? Babies born when Beveridge was outlining his system of social security, as we saw in Chapter 2, could expect to celebrate around 60 birthdays. That is if the mortality rates that existed at their birth remained the same throughout their lifetime. Of course, with the advent of the NHS, those babies enjoyed substantial improvements to mortality rates. In fact, by the time they reached their sixtieth birthday in 2002, increases in life expectancy had risen so that they might enjoy another 20 or so years of life (Office for National Statistics 2021a). At the population level, the benefits of Beveridge's welfare state, particularly the NHS, are truly remarkable. Even for individuals, the extent of provision for welfare established by Beveridge was unprecedented. Improving living conditions through better housing, expanding education and the full-scale attack mounted on poverty stood alongside better and growing access to ever-developing medical interventions. That we now tend to live longer than our great-grandparents is no surprise. But the gains heralded by Beveridge's vision are in danger, while some have already been lost. The collective participation and shared sense of responsibility fanned by the shared trauma of two successive world wars weakened as the neoliberal, capitalist ideologies of

31

contemporary society came to regard welfare as a costly burden. The system has, to invoke Hilary Cottam's (2021) arguments on welfare reform, always been designed with humans imagined as self-interested, self-maximizing individuals. But this has now overtaken any sense of a shared fate in the creation of the system of social security, which is now hollowed out, overburdened and in peril. For some the consequences are severe, whereas for others high incomes, high wealth and high self-esteem are sufficient buffers. To understand the scale of work needed to now launch a new attack on our contemporary and more monstrous giant of Disease, we must understand its uneven pursuit of the population.

UNEQUAL HEALTH

In 2021 a baby boy born in south-east England might live to be 80, but if they were born in Scotland they may not live past 77. What is so different about the experiences of that boy in south-east England from those of that boy in Scotland? It isn't just between countries and regions of the UK that such differences emerge. They also play out between postcodes within cities and regions, often to an astonishing degree. Tracking life expectancy across the tram network of Greater Manchester makes that only too clear: travel less than 20 miles between Stretford and Rochdale and a baby boy might lose as much as ten years from their life expectancy. These differences are also manifest by occupation – just as they were in 1842 – as well as by things like income, education and housing tenure. In August 1980, the publication of the Black Report sparked sustained interest in understanding why inequalities such as these had in fact widened since the creation of an NHS premised on universal access to medical intervention. Medical intervention alone is evidently not enough to safeguard equitable health outcomes for all. Professor Pete Townsend and colleagues, authors of the Black Report, emphasized "the complex effects of the economy and different forms of social organization, including the family, upon levels of health" (Department of Health and Social Security 1980: 8). Paralleling Galtung's (1969) earlier exposition on structural violence, the Black Report focused on what are now commonly referred to as the social determinants of health. It highlighted the corresponding and interacting accumulated disadvantage of some in the population compared to the relative advantage of others. Measured primarily through differences in mortality between social classes (defined by occupation), the report demonstrated a social gradient to health, since labelled as one of the most reliable findings in public health research (Kröger *et al.* 2015: 1). The lower the social class, the poorer the health outcomes. Explanations vary as to why this gradient persists, but the report gave primacy to the material conditions of life. What Galtung construed explicitly as violence, the authors addressed but in less inflammatory terms. Yet in both cases, of significance is the uneven distribution of resources built into the fabric of society which then matters for the conditions in which people are born, grow, live, work and age: the social determinants of health.

It was not until Labour's landslide victory over the Conservative Party in 1997 that efforts to address the concerns espoused in the Black Report began to appear in policy. Labour's interest in health inequality prompted their commission of the now famous Marmot Review, published just three months shy of the surprising formation of a coalition government between the Conservatives and the Liberal Democrats in 2010. The new coalition heralded an abrupt end to policies explicitly tackling inequalities in health as well as the advent of a decade of fiscal austerity in response to the global financial crisis of 2008. Both have had severe consequences for the health of the population, particularly those in ever more strained circumstances. The political and economic landscape of the UK today lays bare the consequences of not only ignoring the social determinants of health but also of the individualization of responsibility for health and the continued rolling back of our welfare state. Covid-19 has a lot to answer for, but it is the social and political determinants of health we must interrogate to understand why.

THE SOCIAL DETERMINANTS OF HEALTH

Who we are and where we live has always mattered for our health and well-being (recall the interests and works of ancient Greece's Hippocrates, or Victorian Britain's Chadwick). Our health, and therefore our life expectancy, is partly shaped by genetics and the nature and extent of medical care. But genetics and indeed medical care play a relatively minor role. Are the genetics of a boy born in Stretford really so different from one born in Rochdale? Of course not. Does their access to medical care really vary so much? In some ways perhaps. But such a distance is unlikely to account for the lost ten years of life. Genetics and medical intervention play a part in determining health and longevity, but the remainder is then a matter of society: how society is structured and what that means for our lives as we age. Beveridge's five giants can start to show us how.

Want, in the contemporary narrative, is the condition of poverty, a state in which people's material resources are not sufficient to meet either their physiological or social needs. To live in poverty, or a state of destitution or privation, matters for health. But it is not just that some people are poor while others are rich that explains the magnitude of differences we see, for example, between the babies of Stretford relative to the babies of Rochdale. There is also the tricky issue of how much poorer, or how much richer, different people in society are relative to each other. Squalor turns attention to the homes and neighbourhoods in which we live. Living in a mouldy, crowded, poorly insulated home is unequivocally risky for your health. But just as it matters how much more money the baby from Stretford may have relative to the baby from Rochdale, even if neither would consider themselves particularly well off, so too do these sorts of graded differences in housing and neighbourhood quality matter. How forgotten would you feel living on an estate with poor transport connections, overflowing bins, broken windows and little beyond the corner shop, bookmakers and bargain off-licence to shop in? Idleness is a matter of (un)employment. Beveridge sought a state of full employment in which 97 per cent of the possible workforce would be in work. But that does not go far enough. We know, for example, that just where you sit in the occupational hierarchy matters a great deal for your health. It's not just having a job but what job you have, how secure your contract is and whether you are treated and paid fairly. Finally, ignorance is concerned with education. It's more than just at what age you left full-time education and with what qualifications. It also matters how we value and think about the different skills, education and training pathways accessible to different groups of society. Returning to Greater Manchester, for example, pupils from more affluent backgrounds are twice as likely to go to university as their less well-off peers in neighbouring areas. Where you are born matters for where you go to school and what sort of education you will receive. This then feeds into all sorts of related decisions or constraints, such as whether you can attend university and where.

It is very easy to turn from Beveridge's giants to different dimensions of the social determinants of health. The conditions in which we are born, grow, work, live and age are inseparable from our material circumstances, our homes, our neighbourhoods, our schooling and our working lives. These different arenas of life shape our income and earnings; they matter for early childhood development and for our feelings of inclusion or exclusion across societal institutions and structures. They matter too for our access to health and social care. It is impossible, then, to discuss Beveridge's giant of Disease without some attention to its comrades in arms. Yet others in this series will turn to them in more depth. What matters here is understanding their relationship with individual- and population-level health and well-being, how they have disrupted progress in tackling disease and how they facilitate its uneven attack on the population.

PLACING POOR HEALTH

Let's travel a few miles from Rochdale and Stretford in Greater Manchester to neighbouring Eccles. In November 2021, after the temporary uplift to universal credit introduced during the early months of Covid-19 was cut, Vicky Gillot was interviewed by a local reporter. "We struggle with food, shopping, heating and electric", she shared. As her private landlord chose to sell up, she must now contend with the struggle to buy basic necessities and the threat of homelessness for her and her children: "I've had to go to the doctors for my mental health" (Oldfield 2021). Although a baby born in Eccles fares better in life expectancy than one born in Rochdale, the picture painted by Vicky and her neighbours is bleak. "The future used to be exciting ... now it's frightening", said 61-year-old local busker Hugh Mortimer. "All of my friends are dying ... two have died in the last two weeks ... you don't get better. You just get worse", said Peter O'Connor, aged 60. What does it mean to be born in such an area? Our lives do not happen in a spatial vacuum.

It matters where we are born as well as who we are born to. You might be born into a relatively poor family, living in a relatively deprived area such as Eccles. But for some that experience of deprivation will not always characterize their entire life. What if you win a scholarship to a local grammar school? What if you had the opportunity to attend a redbrick university? What if you obtain graduate-level employment? Your experiences as you grow, live and work in later life may then be very different from the circumstances you were born into. Although the chances of such a dramatic transformation in the social and economic conditions of one's life are rare, many can and do see relative improvement in their lot over their lifetime. This might be in comparison to the circumstances of their birth or that of their parents. And yet, for countless more, where you are born has an impact on when you will die and everything in between.

The underlying geography to our experiences from birth onwards, and how that shapes transitions between key stages of our lives – leaving education, entering work, family formation and dissolution, parenting and retirement – has a pivotal role in our chances of good health and long lives. Consider again the opportunities for a child born to a relatively poor family living in a relatively deprived area. The labour markets that characterize that local area largely determine what that child's parent(s) may do. This matters for their income, which also matters for what sort of house they live in, the sorts of leisure activities they get up to and what food they eat. Their house, their recreation and their food are all tied up in the characteristics of the area in which they live. Where they live dictates what local services are available, the type and quality of local schools and whether the high street is filled with boutiques or discount stores. But it goes beyond retail and schooling, expanding to things like the health and even social care you have access to. Julian Tudor Hart (1971) famously wrote of the "inverse care law", arguing that the places with the greatest need have the fewest healthcare services. The jury is out on whether and to what extent that law still operates, but if you have ill people with higher demand for a fixed amount of care, this will have an impact on access and use of those services. It might even affect the quality of care available too. Thinking about the relationship between the people that live in a place, and the place that people live in, turns attention to a long-standing debate for health geographers. What is the relative importance of the people or the place in shaping the sorts of differences in health we see between Stretford and Rochdale, or south-east England and Scotland?

To unpack that debate, imagine two fictitious towns – Healthsville and Illton. Rates of mortality in Healthsville are very

low whereas in Illton they are worryingly high. Why? Let's look
at the people who live there. In Healthsville, they are relatively
young and employed in stable, professional occupations. In contrast, people in Illton are much older and many used to work in
factories and now-closed coalmines. This tells us quite a lot about
why there are differences in health between the two towns. A lot
is explained by the social and economic characteristics of the
people who live there. However, we can learn even more if we also
look at the characteristics of the places themselves. Healthsville,
with its young, affluent, employed population, has very good
transport links, lots of green open space and plenty of affordable
grocery stores, leisure centres and good-quality housing. Access
to healthcare is also readily available. Illton is on the coast, with
few transport links, limited social infrastructure and health and
social care services straining under demand. The sorts of services
and amenities available to a local population, and the environment in which they sit, interacts with the people who live there.
Are people educated so as to know when to seek out healthcare?
Have people felt ignored or discriminated against by societal institutions (including healthcare services), which changes when and
why they may choose to engage with them? It is not just the composition of people in places that explains inequalities in health
between places but how the very context of those places interacts
with and shapes the experiences of people living and working in
them. We are moving closer to understanding why a baby born
in south-east England may expect to live longer than a baby born
in Scotland. But it's more than just the people or the places in
which they live and work.

THE POLITICS OF HEALTH

The dominant ideology governing UK politics is that of neoliberalism. Neoliberalism advocates a strong state but only in so
far as this facilitates the state's ability to maintain the primacy

of the market, elevating competition principles as the key mechanism through which to organize society, allocate resources and determine success. Marketization seeps into many aspects of society, including the management of our NHS. It also creates the space for deeply entrenched inequalities that are readily dismissible as the by-product of a system where some compete successfully while others are less able to measure up. It is ironic that the evolution of liberal values has come to this, given that the foundations of such values began with a challenge to the dominant power of aristocracy and the extent to which one's social position was determined through little more than the (mis)fortune of one's birth.

For our purposes, it is worth noting the changes in attitudes to the role and reach of the state in so far as they relate to the different conceptions of the commitment to the individual. Emphasis on the individual is central to liberal ideology, although it manifests itself in different ways. For example, early liberals sought to minimize state interference in private life, leaving the collection of individuals that make up society free to make their own choices predicated on their own distinctive qualities and attributes. Modern liberals, however, though sharing in the commitment to the individual, each with distinctive qualities and attributes, recognize the universality of our status as individuals in society. Coincident with this more egalitarian approach to the individual is acceptance of a stronger state, managing not only the economy but also the provision of welfare services. Human flourishing is prioritized, requiring some level of social responsibility for other individuals in the society we live in. But has that shared sense of social responsibility been lost? Hilary Cottam, among others, would argue it certainly has. And perhaps it was never strong enough to begin with.

Changing liberal attitudes towards the role of the state underpin the changing political and fiscal approaches to welfare provision that have characterized the building up and subsequent dismantling of Beveridge's vision. The rise of the market and the individual has shifted responsibility for health and well-being away from the state. This can be clearly seen in responses to the Covid-19 pandemic. The secretary of state for health, Matt Hancock, called for all overweight people to lose at least 5 lbs to save "countless lives" and "spare" the NHS a cost of £100 million (cited in Donnelly & Rayner 2020). This places responsibility on the individual for their weight, and for the consequences of that weight on the NHS, without addressing the structures in society that mean some are more likely to weigh in heavier than others. Affordable, nutritious food, for example, is just one part of that problem: the rise of in-work poverty and precarious contracts means food can become a luxury they neither have the time to shop for or prepare, nor the finances to meet. But it also pathologizes the fat body and creates a target for stigma. Amid the public anger, fear and frustration of Covid-19, blame is easily moved between thin, acceptable bodies and fat, problematic ones. And with blame, so comes responsibility. For Matt Hancock, this approach was happily in line with his previous arguments to improve healthy life expectancy. Shifting attention away from the failings of either the health and social care system or society at large, he handed the baton of responsibility for society's problems to people themselves: "It's about people choosing to look after themselves better ... Making better choices" (cited in Campbell 2018). In such a society is it any surprise that we police parents and demonize mothers when their children weigh in as "fat", rather than work to dismantle the social and economic structures which increase the risk of fatness in them and their children?

But back to Covid-19. Hard on the heels of these sorts of fat-shaming policy approaches were repeated statements that communities and people were to blame for the return to more stringent lockdown measures imposed on some parts of the country. Residents of northern England were not, according to Hancock, "abiding to social distancing" (cited in Halliday 2020).

Responsibility for rising rates of infection and a mounting death toll were placed on the shoulders of "fat" and dissenting individuals. Where political rhetoric seeks to carve out a gap between state responsibility for the maintenance of the structures that advantage some while suppressing others, and individual experience of those structures, we should condemn this as violence. Where our babies' chances of survival are a matter of whether or not they are born into deprivation, or whether or not they are Black or Brown, we must act. Where the risk of fatness in our children is a matter of how deprived an area they live or school in, we must act.

EXPLAINING UNEQUAL HEALTH

By this point, you are probably reflecting on your personal circumstances and the area in which you live. You might even be wondering about the political structures and their reach into your life. Do they really matter for whether or not you get sick? For if you are low, depressed or anxious? Or for when you will die? There is a wealth of evidence showing that they do, some of which is referenced in these pages. But to give more substance to these arguments, we can turn briefly to some of the theories explaining exactly why one's social position matters so much for health. One argument is that vigour, ability and strength (to borrow the language of the Black Report) naturally elevates people in the social hierarchy, while the less fortunate either remain at or drift towards the bottom. But dismissing inequalities in health as a natural reflection of "innate physical characteristics" is intensely problematic, particularly if we accept – as we should – that health is a social phenomenon. Alternatively, health may determine social position but only indirectly. In other words, it is the influence of different determinants of health that begin to accrue from birth that determine social position. Birth weight, height and nutrition, for example, interact with socioeconomic position and experience of deprivation in childhood and adolescence. The accumulated (dis)advantage matters for later health, later socio-economic position and later deprivation. Over one's lifetime, this could contribute to both upwards and downwards social mobility. It has been widely debated in academic literature whether such social mobility can then widen or narrow inequalities in health. These "selection" effects have also been considered as a mech-anism to explain why inequalities in health between places may change, as well as between people. In these explanations, health (directly or indirectly) determines social position.

Or does social position determine health? The material conditions of one's life are evident in the social and economic structures we inhabit. Some live in poverty whereas others sit somewhere along a relative scale of precarity, stability, comfort or luxury. If you live in a good-quality home you probably live in an area with a good range of services and amenities, and you are probably less likely to be exposed to high levels of air pollution. You can buy nutritious food and have a good education. This good education means you are well positioned in the labour market, can earn a good income and can maintain your wider comfort-able living situation. Short of an unprecedented or unanticipated external shock, you will probably either remain in comfort over your lifetime or see continual improvements with promotions, partnerships and rising earnings. The less exposure anyone has to hazardous living or working conditions, the better the chances of good health. As material conditions improve, so too does one's ability to participate fully in society through associated changes in relative power, prestige and social connections. For those at the bottom of the pile, it is easy to see why the consequences of low income may interact with experiences in all other social and eco-nomic arenas of life, cumulatively leading to poor health. Where the extent of our material circumstances also matters for our par-ticipation in and experience of the society we work in, as it does in the UK and many other high-income countries, we will then see a gradient to health outcomes emerge, as the work of Professor Michael Marmot has shown (2005). The material conditions of our work and differences in exposure to industrial hazards in the workplace are important, but so too is the position of an employee relative to others in their workplace or wider sector, as well as the social conditions in which they work.

Although absolute and relative material conditions are undeniably important, some may look to the differences in behaviours between social groups as a means to absolve wider social or political responsibility for them. For anyone wanting to justify the rolling back of the welfare state, this may be attractive. That health inequalities have widened despite the existence of the NHS is not because of insufficient funds or failed interventions. It is the fault of the individual who smokes, who drinks, who takes drugs, who does not exercise or who does not get their "five a day". To explain inequalities in health between social groups as such assumes both that different social groups are differently able to make informed health-related choices and that differences in what is considered acceptable behaviour and normal practice exist between social groups. More emphasis, however, should be given to social context. We do not live in a social or spatial vacuum, nor do we make our life choices in one. Diet is a good example of this. If you have a low income, work long hours and live in an area with limited access to affordable, healthy food, serving beige freezer food for tea should not be construed as a poor life choice. It is a product of the rigid hierarchical structures of the society you live in.

The paragraphs above variously capture different elements of explanations for inequalities in health based on selection effects, or materialist, psychosocial, life course and behavioural-cultural approaches. Life course approaches are particularly illuminating through their emphasis on the timing of exposure to adverse or positive conditions in our lives. Championed by epidemiologists such as Dianah Kuh and Yoav Ben-Shlomo (1997), a life course approach can be understood in two ways. It can either emphasize

exposure to hazardous environments during particularly significant periods of development (e.g. childhood), known as the
critical periods model, or it may favour the accumulation of exposures over time, in which certain exposures at particular points of
development may have a greater impact than others. Whatever
explanation you look to, inequality is self-perpetuating. It gets
under our skin, as Professors Richard Wilkinson and Kate Pickett argue. Not only is the burden of social, economic and health
problems greater in more unequal societies, but "living in a more
unequal society changes how we think and feel and how we relate
to each other" (2018: xvii). In societies with rigid and steep hierarchical structures, people are more likely to compare their lot
with that of others around them. Unfavourable comparisons
further fragment society and have deleterious consequences for
health. Higher rates of emotional disorders, mental illness and
poor physical health are associated with living in more unequal
societies for all. But for those towards the bottom of that rigid
hierarchy, the burden is heavier.

SYNDEMICS AND COVID-19

To live in inner-city Hartford, Connecticut, in the early 1990s
was to be no stranger to hardship. One of the poorest cities of its
size in the United States, with one of the highest levels of crime,
the Puerto Ricans who lived there suffered most. Low incomes,
welfare assistance, single-parent households and low levels of
education marked Puerto Rican migrant communities out from
their African American or white neighbours. Who you are and
where you live matters for your health and well-being. But for
some, like those Puerto Rican communities of Hartford, the burden inflicted by the social, economic, environmental and political
contexts of their lives is even more lethal. Merril Singer (1996)
coined the concept of a "syndemic" to make sense of the health
crisis faced by the Puerto Ricans of Hartford. He argued that the

level of substance abuse, violence and AIDS found in their community could not be viewed as distinct problems or through the lens of comorbidity. Syndemics, he argued, can help us make sense of illnesses that are exacerbated by the context of people's lives. Not only do you have mutually enhancing, often co-occurring health problems running rife in a population, but in a syndemic this is amplified by the "context of a perpetuating configuration of noxious social conditions" (Singer 1996: 99). The toxic social, economic and political conditions which, as we have seen, themselves maintain and exacerbate inequalities in health leave some inexcusably worse off. Syndemics can then be understood as the lethal consequences of structural violence, which are only comprehendible through contemporary biosocial models of health that give weight to the social determinants of health. They are, perhaps, ever more likely in a world in which polarized societies, corrupt power and unequal chances are depressingly common. In the context of the UK, a syndemic's framework, with particular attention to the underlying structural violence, helps us to unpack, for example, why the impacts of Covid-19 were so unevenly felt.

A climate of austerity, rising precarity and the associated declines in health meant that although all were caught up in the global pandemic, for some it was experienced as a syndemic. Relatively modest tax increases alongside major spending cuts characterized the UK approach to the fiscal austerity prompted by the global financial crisis in 2008. The intention was to reduce the budget deficit and thereby stimulate economic growth as confidence in the economy increased. The deficit did fall, but the intended economic growth did not materialize. In fact, the economy stagnated as the cost of living increased. At the same time, widespread cuts to state spending saw significant reductions in social security: the safety net woven by Beveridge, at a time when many needed it the most, was being slowly unpicked. This has been linked to stalling and falling life expectancy, as we discuss further in Chapter 7. But in places, it will have also contributed to the noxious social conditions already increasing vulnerability to a range of chronic health conditions. Covid-19 hit socially and economically disadvantaged communities the hardest. "They had underlying health conditions" was the excuse used by too many politicians or journalists when reporting the latest daily death toll. This is never an acceptable excuse, but it is particularly problematic when the chances of having an underlying chronic health condition are so unevenly and unjustly distributed in the population. Areas of high deprivation, with communities already marginalized in societal structures, had higher rates of infection, the infections were more severe and the outcomes more often fatal. The consequences were racially patterned. It is not only Asian or Black people in Britain who live in deprivation and disadvantage, but those sorts of living and working conditions disproportionately reflect the experiences of minoritized ethnic groups in the UK. Professor Clare Bambra (2020) was among the first to pick up the syndemic framework and apply it to the unequal experiences of the UK, building on her long-standing interest in the political economy of health and inequality. This syndemic framework allows us to interrogate the heightened vulnerability of particular populations in particular places to specific diseases. At the same time, it exposes the politics of these noxious conditions through which some people and places are expendable while others are worthy of investment and power.

This is an undeniably gloomy end to the chapter, but the gloom has a purpose. A *Lancet* special issue on syndemics, some years before the onslaught of Covid-19, concluded in its opening editorial that "in the pursuit of practising more socially conscious medicine, syndemics suggest context is key" (The Lancet 2017: 881). Structural violence, and the syndemics it permits, are a very real plague on society. The politics of the individual, the emphasis on self-interest and the indifference to inequality so long as you have that bit more than the person next to you, creates the space into which structural violence creeps and inequalities take hold. No attempt to reignite the passion and enthusiasm for revival, growth, prosperity and hope Beveridge invoked should begin without recognition of the violence of the structures it must contend with, the inequalities they maintain and the incompatibility of both with the welfare system we need for today. Too many of the gains in health and well-being first heralded by Beveridge's remarkable vision have been lost to the structural violence that has taken root in our systems. We don't need to conjure new giants to address this. We need to understand the make-up of existing ones and understand what facilitates their uneven pursuit of the population. That is how we identify their weakness and learn to bring them down.

4

From cradle . . .

Beveridge's report led to the creation of a social safety net woven to protect us all from cradle to grave. The social and economic advances this heralded were a boon to the health and well-being of the population. Infectious disease, although not altogether eradicated, rescinded and lifespans extended. But complacency and hubris set in. Humankind's encroachment on our fragile global ecosystem has enabled disease vectors to emerge or gain new strength, and we have become blind to the consequences of the social production of health in an uneven, polarizing social system. These consequences extend across the life course but are most damning at the cradle. The penalties to health and longevity imposed on our (unborn) children because of things like their postcode, ethnicity and class are a structural violence. Life expectancy is often viewed as the ultimate marker of health. Is it then the ultimate injustice if there are inequalities in chances of survival to even your first or fifth birthday? Such inequalities in chances of life itself are a very good place to begin this chapter's review of the health and well-being of the children of today. A compromised start in life is a strong predictor of sustained disadvantage in health, well-being and social and economic outcomes. Surviving childhood and adolescence is not enough to safeguard against the ills of tomorrow. Our discussion of the rising prevalence of childhood obesity and adolescent mental health problems will lay bare the catastrophe of tomorrow foretold by the health and well-being crises of today.

INFANT AND CHILD MORTALITY

Globally as many as 15,000 children under the age of five die every day. In low- and middle-income countries, infectious diseases claim the lives of countless children (pneumonia is among the leading causes of death). Limited access to appropriate maternity and paediatric healthcare reduces opportunities to treat and prevent the spread of infectious disease in many countries. Poor living conditions, including a lack of clean water and food, only serve to worsen the death toll. But in high-income countries such as the UK, where relatively few live in a state of privation, deaths of children are not as rare as we might expect. The UK, like many other high-income countries, experienced large declines in infant mortality rates (measured as the number of children who die before their first birthday per 1,000 live births) during the latter half of the twentieth century and into the twenty-first. In 1942, 49 babies in England, around 56 in Wales and just under 70 for Scotland died before their first birthday for every 1,000 live births. By 2019 this had dropped dramatically. In England and Scotland, it had fallen to four babies and only three in Wales. The scale of this decline, and the change seen in Northern Ireland from 1971, is cause for celebration (see Figure 4.1). This improvement is driven to a large extent by the healthcare provided in our welfare state and, of course, the changes in living standards that its introduction and wider socioeconomic development ensured.

But now, despite these gains and universal healthcare across the UK, we lag behind our peers in other high-income countries. To die from a preventable cause before you reach your first or fifth birthday is tragic. But this tragedy is made violent when the chances of your death increase, in a country with the resources to prevent this, simply because of where you were born and who you

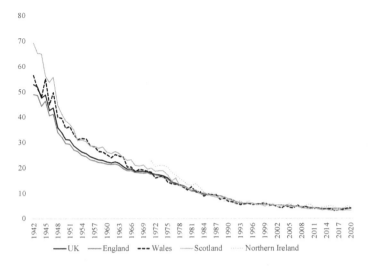

Figure 4.1 Infant mortality rate per 1,000 live births, UK, 1942–2019

Source: Office for National Statistics (2021b).

were born to. Not only are rates of infant mortality higher in the UK when compared to other high-income countries, the social gradient of those deaths is also steeper. This means that in the UK it matters more where you are born and where you are in the social hierarchy than it does in other comparable countries. Figure 4.2 (indicating England's infant mortality rate) shows that the infant mortality rate is higher than the average for England for those born into the most deprived areas. Similarly, families in the least deprived areas have significantly lower infant mortality rates. This pattern is repeated in more recent data in England and reproduced across the UK (Odd *et al.* 2021). Not only is there a persistent gap between more and less deprived places, recent infant mortality rates for babies born to mothers living in the most deprived or most disadvantaged circumstances have actually begun to increase.

Since 2016, Scotland has seen a rise in infant mortality for the

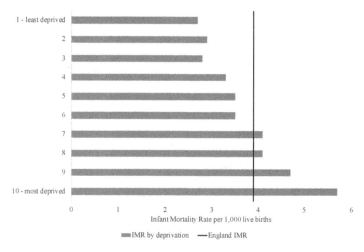

Figure 4.2   Infant mortality rate by deprivation, England, 2018–20

Source: Public Health England (n.d.).

most disadvantaged groups (Harpur *et al.* 2021). England, too, experienced a sustained and unprecedented rise in infant mortality from 2014, countering previous declines in infant mortality in the most deprived places (Taylor-Robinson *et al.* 2019). For every 1 per cent increase in child poverty, this means an estimated additional 5.8 infant deaths per 100,000 live births. The silence on this issue can only be explained by our complacency. There are 4.3 million children living in poverty across the UK (2019–20) and counting. We, and our politicians, are taking the previous generations' gains for granted, yet the evidence shows it should be otherwise. The rise in child poverty matters for more than just a baby's chances of life or death. It also matters for the development trajectories of those who survive and continues to shape their health, social and economic outcomes into adulthood. It is worth highlighting that although many living in a deprived area are in some way poor, this isn't necessarily true of all. However, the social patterning of infant mortality is not only apparent by area deprivation but also between socioeconomic groups. Data from the Office for National Statistics group infant mortality rates between 2011 and 2017 according to three tiers of socioeconomic group. Those towards the top of the social hierarchy have the lowest rates of infant mortality. The gaps are consistent over time (see Figure 4.3).

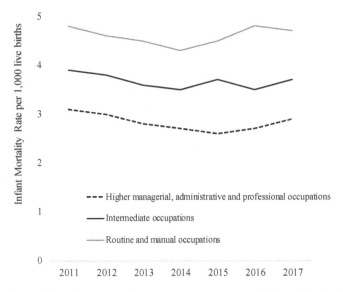

Figure 4.3   Infant mortality rate by socioeconomic class, England and Wales, 2011–17

Source: Office for National Statistics (2019).

The consistency of the social patterning of infant mortality over time is a clear indicator of the need for greater and more targeted investment in maternal health and well-being facilities for mums-to-be during and after pregnancy. The data raise the question of why mothers in more deprived areas, or in lower socioeconomic groups, seem to have higher chances of preterm birth and higher chances of losing their baby. The Office for National Statistics suggests that the differences are attributable to differences in smoking and breastfeeding, without additional reflection on "the causes of the causes" (to invoke the likes of Professor Michael Marmot). Although the data analysts at the Office for National Statistics do point to the link between levels of deprivation and poor maternal health – alongside the consequences of smoking in pregnancy and decision to breastfeed – this is still deceptive as to the causal role of uneven power structures, inequality and political and economic neglect. We should promote healthy choices for women during pregnancy, but we should not be blind to the reasons behind unhealthy choices, the factors that constrain or enable those choices and the consequences of structural violence. Some readers may recall their mothers being frowned upon for choosing to breastfeed, a signal of their poverty and inability to buy the superior formula. This is quite clearly a triumph of marketing and an indicator of the sometimes erroneous consequences of the medicalization of childbirth since Beveridge's day at the expense of generations of maternal knowledge. Social attitudes play a hugely significant role in the context of maternal health and bringing up our children, which is a crucial consideration for their health and well-being, and the provisions of a welfare state.

The rise in infant mortality in England has now been attributed to deaths of babies born after less than 24 weeks of gestation (Nath *et al.* 2021). Some may then look to the timings of infant mortality as a means to explain away their significance. We should emphatically resist this. Medical advances perhaps mean that a foetus, which may once have been lost in the early stages of gestation, survives for a longer period. But when some of those are then lost, and the chances of that loss increases if you are more disadvantaged, this cannot be ignored. Infant mortality is a signal of major concern in the health and well-being of the population.

It is also a signal for potential further adverse trends. It is telling, then, that the rise in infant mortality seen was not only coincident with the stalling and falling of life expectancy more generally, pre-pandemic, but also that the improvements we had enjoyed previously to infant mortality have themselves stalled.

Despite the bleak picture painted here, there has been progress, as documented by the Royal College of Paediatrics and Child Health (2020) in their "State of Child Health" reports. For example, between 2017 and 2020, the rate of mortality (defined as the number of children who die out of every 100,000 children) for children aged between one and nine has decreased in England, Wales and Northern Ireland, as has the rate of adolescent mortality (ages 10–19). In Scotland, however, despite having the lowest rates of both infant and child mortality across the UK, their rates of child and adolescent mortality are on the rise. By 2020, nearly 25 out of every 100,000 adolescents died. This is, as you might have guessed, unevenly distributed across the country. Indeed, that uneven geography extends across the UK, as seen in Figure 4.4. In Scotland, the rates are highest in South Ayrshire, one of the most deprived regions of Scotland and an area where nearly a quarter of its children are living in poverty.

If the children of today are the future of tomorrow, rising mortality, stalling improvements and unjust differences should be things that everyone has a vested interest in addressing. Despite a free, universal health service, the existence of a welfare system designed to provide social security and relative economic prosperity overall, the UK continues to perform poorly in deaths among children. Relatively high rates of infant deaths, and deaths among children and young people with chronic conditions, all of which are socially patterned, sit alongside a crisis in our provision for children, especially for children in need. At worse, this can lead to avoidable deaths.

Given that these deaths are socially patterned, points of intervention are readily identifiable. Some may be thinking that if

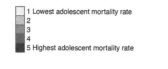

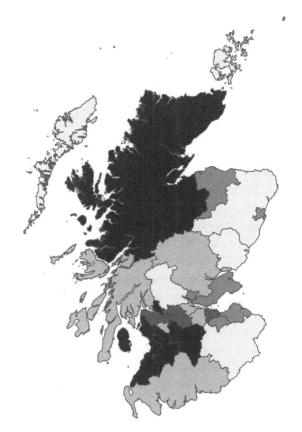

Figure 4.4   Map of adolescent mortality, Scotland, local area, 2019

Source: National Records of Scotland (2019).

parents cannot parent, the children should be taken into care. At times, this may be the best course of action, particularly as the main reasons children are taken into care is because of abuse and neglect. But our care system is under immense pressure, with the number of children taken into care growing at a faster rate than the UK child population. Sadly, children in care also tend to have poorer physical and mental health outcomes than those not in care. Wholesale change to how we support struggling parents, and children in need, is evidently needed. Parents are best able to provide for their children and maximize their health chances when they themselves are supported in education and lifelong learning, occupied in meaningful employment with secure, stable incomes, and living in good-quality accommodation in a good-quality wider environment. It should be impossible to dismiss that the risk of death for a baby born to a mother living in the most deprived areas of the country is 94 per cent higher than it would be if they were born to a mother living in the least deprived areas (Nath *et al.* 2021). The structures of society maintain inequalities in outcomes and experience that cannot be maligned as the fault or consequence of poor lifestyle choices. By accepting this social stratification as a given, we are complicit in the violence against these babies, and ultimately we are culpable for turning a blind eye.

To live, then, in the north of England, for example, is to risk poorer health outcomes and a shorter life than someone living in England's south. Across the UK, the risk for those living in deprivation, or by those who belong to less advantaged social groups, is greater than that of those in more affluent situations. We can, however, find even starker evidence of the violent structures of our society. To be Black or Brown in the UK is to shoulder an additional penalty and one that begins even before you are born. If your parents are poorer, working in low-pay, low-value, insecure work, living in precarious, unsuitable or overcrowded housing, with lower levels of education, the odds are already

stacked against you. Poverty, deprivation and precarity during
pregnancy all matter for your future development. This shapes the
chances of being born preterm, being stillborn and whether you
are a healthy weight. In England, for example, one study estimated
that 24 per cent of stillbirths would not have happened were the
risks to women living in the most deprived areas the same as
those in the least deprived areas (Jardine *et al.* 2021). But the number would reduce further should the risks to women of colour be
the same as the risks to women from a white ethnic background.
An earlier study in England and Wales also concluded that ethnic
minority babies had an up to 138 per cent greater risk of death
or preterm birth compared to white British babies (Opondo *et al.*
2019). And it's not just the babies that are at risk. Asian and Black
women are more likely to die in pregnancy than white women. It is
a symptom of the uneven power structures and systematic biases
institutionalized in the fabric of British society that your race and
your social position at conception determine your life chances
so completely.

More than four million children live in poverty in the UK, a
number that has risen dramatically since 2014. As you would
expect, the patterning to child poverty traces existing social,
economic and political fault lines in society. But it is also racially
patterned. Pre-pandemic, rates of child poverty were notably
lower among white British children than for ethnic minorities:
17 per cent of white British children lived in poverty; this climbs
to 30 per cent for Black children, 31 per cent for Chinese children and 33 per cent for children with a mixed ethnicity, and is
as high as 41 per cent for Bangladeshi children and 47 per cent
for Pakistani children (Office for National Statistics 2020c). In
fact, children in Asian households are 2.5 times as likely to live
in persistent poverty relative to the national average. The government's 2021 Commission on Race and Ethnic Disparities
concluded "ironically", according to the foreword from the chair,
that very few of the disparities between ethnic and racial groups,

such as differences in birth outcomes, are attributable to racism. But is that true? Neither differences in socioeconomic background, nor indeed differences in genetic make-up (which are in fact marginal), adequately explain differences in health outcomes for ethnic minorities. Although socioeconomic background is an important and significant part of the picture, we should not ignore the additional penalty of ethnicity and the consequences of discrimination. Nor should we ignore the implicit bias evident in societal structures and opportunities where ethnic minorities are more likely than white British to live in deprivation, precarity and poverty.

Being subjected to racial discrimination has a profound effect on both physical and mental health outcomes for ethnic minorities. For mothers, this has further adverse consequences for their unborn children's socioemotional development. The consequences of a racist slur and the repeated microaggressions in your day-to-day life are not insignificant. But where institutions are at worst racist, or at best biased, the combined affect at the individual and institutional levels can be catastrophic. The NHS, like society, is biased towards the white British majority group. And, just as racialized assumptions about people's abilities and characteristics shape bias in education, access to the housing market, job interviews and career progression, so too do those sorts of assumptions shape approaches to healthcare. Indeed, many of these themes are covered in more depth in the wider series. But here, a common example to consider is the perception that Black and Asian women have a low pain threshold. This can influence treatment and care in times of trauma, including birth. The bias of individuals and their assumptions, which have been seen to inform clinical decision-making, also seeps into the algorithms and tools used in healthcare to support triage, diagnosis and treatment. We import our bias into the code and engineering of such equipment. Although unintentional, the consequences can lead to poorer health outcomes, inappropriate care and even death. A notable example of such bias was exposed by the Covid-19 pandemic. Equipment used to measure oxygen levels in blood – a key indicator of the severity of Covid-19 – simply did not work as well on darker skin. To be born into socioeconomic disadvantage, into a society that discriminates against you and your parents because of the colour of your skin, is to begin your life at a disadvantage. It can, as noted above, impact your socioemotional development while also compromising your chances of achieving and maintaining good physical and mental health as you age and grow. It is surely imperative that we dismantle the structures through which the violence of deprivation, poverty, inequality and racism continue to limit the chances of our unborn children.

THE CRISIS OF OBESITY

What did you eat for breakfast? And for tea? If I were to pose that question to the people of 1942, the scope and scale of their answers would be remarkably different from the answers I might get today. Today, breakfast may be anything from toast, to cereal, to the famed "full English" (or regional equivalent), whereas options for tea (or dinner) are perhaps endless. This was certainly not the case in 1942, when food rationing and limited and disrupted supply chains decided what was on the table. An adult's weekly ration would, by today's standards, look meagre. For example, the average packet of bacon in the supermarket today is 350g; this might, for the carnivorous among us, do one person over a week. But rations allocated little more than 100g of ham or bacon per person per week in the years *after* the war. Children too had their food rationed but were allocated more of the things considered key to their nutritional development: children got more than the one fresh egg rationed to an adult per week. But this was not enough to stave off diseases of nutrition deficiency, which were on the rise through the consequences of the war. Today, however, diseases of nutrition are more often about excess. Since

1975, the WHO reports that obesity has nearly tripled worldwide. Thirty-nine million children under the age of five, and 340 million children and adolescents up to the age of 19, were overweight or obese in 2016 and 2020 (World Health Organization 2021). The scale of this is no less staggering in the UK.

In Scotland, estimates for 2019/20 suggest that nearly a quarter of a million children aged two to 15 were at risk of excess weight, 131,000 of which were at risk of obesity (Obesity Action Scotland 2021). Although this number has not really changed in the last decade or so, the gap between the richer and poorer children of society has increased. By 2019/20, whereas 17 per cent of children living in the least deprived areas were at risk of excess weight, this climbed to 27 per cent of children living in the most deprived areas (Public Health Scotland 2020). This patterning to risk of excess weight is replicated across the UK. For example, more than a quarter of children are classified as overweight or obese in Northern Ireland and Wales, but the chances of excess of weight are higher in more deprived areas (Public Health Wales NHS Trust 2019). In England, too, the gap between poor and rich children has widened over time, as exemplified for children in the last year of primary school in Figure 4.5. In England, these same inequalities are also found between ethnic groups. For example, the relative increase in prevalence of obesity or severe obesity was greater for Black and Asian children than among white children (Sinha *et al.* 2021). UK-wide strategies to combat childhood obesity have clearly failed; so much so that we have also seen the introduction of a new category of weight in National Childhood Measurement Programmes of "severe obesity".

Obesity is one of the most intractable health challenges of contemporary society. In our exploration of progress under Beveridge's welfare state and the consequences of structural violence, the question of obesity is acutely significant. To be fat in contemporary society is to be stigmatized. Fatness is associated with poor lifestyle choices, laziness and responsibility for the assumed

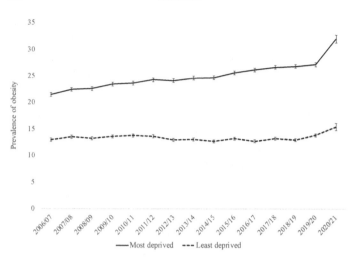

Figure 4.5   Prevalence of obesity, children in last year of primary school, England, 2006/07–2020/21

Source: National Child Measurement Programme (NHS Digital 2021).

Note: The data for 2006/07 to 2008/09 is probably an underestimate because of low participation.

consequences for wider health outcomes. Parents of fat children are then to be criticized and vilified, particularly given what this fatness means for their children's development and health experiences as an adolescent, young adult and beyond. The WHO lists the consequences of childhood obesity, including suffering from high blood pressure and metabolic disorders as a child or obesity and cardiovascular disease as an adult. It can also as much as quadruple the risk of developing Type 2 diabetes as an adult (Abbasi *et al.* 2017).

Childhood obesity also matters for socioemotional experiences, risking lower self-esteem and increasing the likelihood of being bullied. Excess weight is also associated with poorer outcomes in school which, in turn, can lead to poorer outcomes as an adult in the labour market. It is difficult not to see the logic in addressing the chances of childhood obesity. But any discussion of obesity and health has to be approached with some caution, particularly if we subscribe to social models of health. The prevailing narrative within medical and public health circles is that of an obesity epidemic plaguing high-income countries, including the UK. Obesity is pathologized, inducing a fear of fatness, which shifts attention away from the potential responsibilities of the state and society for poor health outcomes to the shoulders of the individual. Imagine being a single parent, working multiple precarious low-paid jobs with erratic and variable shifts, trying to make ends meet. Your time is limited, as is your ability (and probably space) to stock up on foodstuffs over a week to prepare nutritious, filling meals. How easy is it to turn to the local takeaway or to quick oven-ready freezer food? How easy is it for you to ensure your child has a balanced breakfast every day? Are you able to be there when they leave for school or are you already at work? As we condemn and blame parents for the choices foisted on them, free school meals have become stigmatized to the point that getting parents to claim their entitlement has become a regular undertaking for schools. Some children would rather skip lunch than risk the teasing and bullying inflicted on those using the vouchers in the school canteen. The social and economic structures of our society constrain options for parents with fewer resources and increase vulnerability for their children. Given what we know about the impacts of our unjust and violent societal structures, let alone the costs that can be associated with maintaining a healthy, balanced diet, should we not accept some blame for the circumstances in our society that have led to its increasing weight? And yet, the prevailing narrative is that to be fat and in poor health is to be responsible for that poor health (or the poor health of your child), regardless of what other causes may be important (or the actual health of you or your child).

What exactly then is a healthy weight for a growing child?

The metrics informing the categories of "overweight", "obese" and "severe obesity" are themselves problematic. The validity of the body mass index, a widely used metric for weight, has been called into question. These sorts of debates rarely accompany discussions of fatness (or obesity) in the context of population health. Rather than looking at the violence of social stratification harming society, or the political choices made to cut back our welfare state, we blame parents and "fat" bodies. Narrow, inherently biomedical approaches to body weight ignores the complexity of the interrelationships between adverse health outcomes, body weight and the fabric and structures of contemporary society. Because chances of excess weight (at whatever threshold that becomes harmful to an individual) are patterned by deprivation and ethnicity, the problem lies at the societal level. Rather than any interrogation, condemnation or policing of individuals alone, we should demand action where societal structures not only increase the risk of obesity in childhood but simultaneously undermine the ability of our parents to adequately provide for the nutritional needs of their children. Covid-19 catapulted debates over the provision of free school meals into the headlines. The government may wish to strategize (futilely) over tackling childhood obesity, but when it came to ensuring children receive proper and adequate nutrition in a time of crisis, it shied away from its responsibility. We do of course have a role to play in our own weight and that of our children. But when the focus is on the failings of an individual or of a parent alone when we see a fat body, we ignore the culpability of poverty, deprivation, precarity and inequality.

MENTAL HEALTH

The WHO, as noted above, draws out the implications of fatness in childhood on self-esteem and on the likelihood of being bullied. Excess weight has also been associated with a wider set of psychological problems, including depression and anxiety, although whether fatness in children causes depression or vice versa remains unclear. Nevertheless, attention to the mental toll of obesity (and the policing and stigmatizing of fatness) in children also illuminates the heavy burden of mental health problems for our children and adolescents more generally. Globally, depression and anxiety are among the leading contributors to the global health-related burden. In other words, no small part of what ails us around the world is defined by depression and anxiety. Covid-19 did nothing to alleviate this, and the impact on children has been sizeable. Pre-pandemic, the well-being of children and young people across the UK was low compared to many other countries, with evidence suggesting levels are decreasing further (UNICEF Innocenti 2016). But, unsurprisingly, poor well-being is not evenly distributed. Children with special educational needs, children and young people living with a disability, poorer children and young people, and some from ethnic minority groups, are more anxious than other children and young people. Yet across the UK, although need and demand for support services to children and young people suffering from poor mental health has increased, the funding and provision has not. A decade of fiscal austerity saw cuts and closures, with little regard to the impact on those already struggling. Privately funded support services are costly and only accessible to the more fortunate or prosperous in society. But if the chances of adverse mental health are greater for children growing up in families with fewer resources, the scale of unmet need and the social and spatial patterning to this will be undeniably staggering. Although demand has increased across the UK for children and adolescent mental health services (CAMHS), funding has stagnated, with funds falling by nearly £500 million since 2013 (Local Government Association 2019). But wait times for those who are referred are sizeable:

> The waiting list for CAMHS is ridiculous. You've got to be well up there on the scale to get referred. Someone with

a little bit of anxiety is not going to get put through to
CAMHS, whereas that anxiety will just carry on getting
worse and worse and worse, and then you end up with
someone with real mental-health issues. (Frontline staff,
cited in Perry *et al*. 2021: 5)

Child and adolescent psychologist Dr Elaine Lockhart warned
that many would not be seen in time to prevent avoidable mental
health issues becoming entrenched by adulthood (Hill 2021). And
even those who do make it into the system are failed because of
complicated, disconnected service delivery:

I'm facing this maze full of doors and every time I open a
door, there's another door, sets of doors. There's no coher-
ent structure within the system that says, Here's a person
who is asking for help, who's engaging with everything
that we're giving, can we please pull this together so we
can actually provide the help that this person needs. (Individual with lived experience of multiple complex needs,
cited in Perry *et al.* 2021: 5)

To begin life on the back foot, to risk adverse health outcomes
and to develop and grow in a time of mental instability and precarity is to begin a life of hardship. For children and young people,
most mental health problems start by the age of 14. Why then has
funding for CAMHS stagnated? Mental health, according to government reports, is the "single largest cause of disability in the UK,
contributing up to 22.8 per cent of the total burden" (Department
of Health n.d.). This outstrips both cancer and cardiovascular disease and costs the economy in England alone up to £105.2 billion
a year. It is incredibly short-sighted to disinvest support services
for our children and adolescents, baking in poor mental health to
the adult population. This interacts with and exacerbates wider
inequality given the uneven risk of poor mental health already

present. As the children of today are exposed to ever more stressors for their mental health – to say nothing of the toxicity of social media – ensuring their well-being and providing adequate support is critical.

So what now? Beveridge's vision of welfare support from the cradle has been decimated by fiscal austerity. In England, this crisis was particularly acute, with the Royal College of Midwives reporting temporary closures to maternity units as well as reductions to services such as parent classes and bereavement support (2016). At the same time, midwifery across the UK has severe staffing pressures, whether because of the ageing workforce of midwives in Scotland or stagnating pay more generally. Staffing shortages, the Royal College of Midwives warns, risks a mass exodus of midwifery staff unwilling to work when they cannot provide safe care (2021). As the complexity of births increases, the situation will worsen without targeted and sustained investment. Such investment must extend beyond maternity services, addressing overwhelmed mental health services and reinstating losses to youth services more generally. In Cardiff, for example, youth service funding was cut by 64 per cent under austerity and was lost entirely in places like Trafford (YMCA 2020). The impact of dismantling the support network created by these sorts of services reveals itself through rising infant mortality rates, the obesity crisis and the mental health epidemic faced by our children and young people. These examples are the tip of the iceberg. They are striking examples of conditions of poor health and poor well-being in childhood and adolescence that can have a severe and long reach into adulthood, all worsened by the social, economic and political structures of society. For those who were born as the welfare state took shape, however, the issues take a different shape. Let us now turn to the end of the life course and the issues of the health of our ageing population.

5

... to grave: the problem of age

The gradual retreat of Beveridge's attack on want, squalor, ignorance, idleness and disease has been cloaked by the principle of fairness: "Where is the fairness, we ask, for the shift-worker, leaving home in the dark hours of the early morning, who looks up at the closed blinds of their next-door neighbour sleeping off a life on benefits?" (Hamnett 2013: 499), to quote the Conservative-led coalition's George Osborne as a compelling example of the political appropriation of the concept of fairness. Such pronouncements are deliberate efforts to incite anger towards the lazy benefit scrounger living comfortably off the back of your hard-earned taxes in order to justify scaling back or cutting benefit payments in general.

The Labour Party, too, were guilty of maligning benefit recipients, building their approach to welfare reform on the USA's "Welfare to Work" legislation that made benefit provision conditional on job-seeking (Hamnett 2013). With the introduction of austerity, this approach escalated. Cutting and capping benefits while tightening eligibility criteria forced many into low-paid, precarious work. At the same time, public services were scaled back or lost. We saw examples of this in Chapter 4: cuts amounted to 750 closed youth centres, 4,500 youth work jobs lost, temporary closures of maternity units and severe wait times for mental health support. For the working-age group, the structural violence of austerity has been condemned as social murder: more people died from malnutrition, more homeless people died on the streets and for every 10,000 work capability assessments completed there were six more suicides (Grover 2019).

The reach of this violence extends far beyond the working ages. Although many older people, through the pension triple lock, were protected against any real-term loss to their state pension and assured that it would, as a minimum, increase in line with inflation, austerity was just as lethal for the less advantaged pensioners. The impact can only be construed as structural violence, which is present when violence is "built into the structure [of society] and shows up as unequal power and consequently as unequal life chances" (Galtung 1969: 171). It is evident that our welfare state is now failing. It is failing our children, it fails our workforce and it is failing our ageing population.

According to the Office for National Statistics life expectancy calculator, I currently have an average life expectancy of 88 years with a one in ten chance of reaching 100. The odds of my reaching a century, and even of living to 88, are far greater for me than they would have been for my great-grandparents. There are contemporary challenges to our likely longevity. Here we look to the implications of expanding lifespans for the experience of disease in a structurally violent society. And, given our tendency as a population to have fewer children, we will also reflect on what the resulting ageing of the population means for welfare responses to the uneven burden of disease in later life.

A RISING BURDEN

Caring for an aged and ageing population raises challenges that Beveridge did not have to contend with. Specifically, the older you get, the more likely it is that you will suffer from multiple chronic health conditions – known as multimorbidity – and from comorbidity. In comorbidity, one condition – the primary or index condition – tends to take precedence. The rising prevalence of two conditions complicates health and social delivery, with multi-morbidity often requiring frequent and sustained interaction with generalists in primary care. Across the UK, multimorbidity is expected to increase, with estimates suggesting that not only will it affect two-thirds of all adults aged 65 and over by 2035, but that the number living with four or more chronic conditions will have doubled by then (NIHR 2018). Although its prevalence does increase with age, already more than one in four primary care patients aged 18 and over in England are reported to live with multimorbidity (Cassel *et al.* 2018). And in Scotland more than half of people living with multimorbidity were found to be younger than 65 (Barnett *et al.* 2012). The threat to later health and well-being to those multimorbid younger age groups is significant, not least because the clinical attention to multimorbidity sits within the work of geriatricians. Multimorbidity complicates care needs, increasing the risks and lengths of hospitalizations, and ultimately lowers people's quality of life. To live with even just one chronic health condition is a burden, but quality of life is poorer, and risk of functional decline or death is greater, for those living with multimorbidity. For older people, multimorbidity is further complicated because of the interaction with comorbidity and frailty and the regular use of five or more medications, otherwise known as polypharmacy (Yarnall *et al.* 2017). The regular use of multiple medications is itself a risk for older people. Not only is polypharmacy associated with functional decline, but the combined use of different medications can lead to adverse interactions between them while individual medications may not work as they should.

Increasing hypertension, depression or anxiety and chronic pain are driving some of the wider population-level increases in multimorbidity. For older people, dementia is also common to the experience of multimorbidity, and research is underway at the University of Sheffield to establish whether the combined influence of ageing and multimorbidity matters for the onset and progression of dementia. Across the UK there are nearly 900,000 people living with dementia. By 2040, we can expect to see an increase of around 100 per cent in the number of people living with severe dementia for all countries of the UK and an increase of as much as 126 per cent in Northern Ireland (Wittenburg *et al.* 2019). The costs of this are staggering, very little of which is associated with healthcare. It is social care and, critically, unpaid care which account for more than 80 per cent of those costs. It is notable that as the number of chronic health conditions an individual suffers from increases, so does the likelihood that one or more relates to mental illness. There are therefore cost implications to the rising prevalence of multimorbidity, just as there are for the rising prevalence of dementia. For individuals, as multimorbidity is associated with increased used of health and social care, not only will this increase the costs of an individual living with multimorbidity, the cost incurred may be greater because of the existence of multiple conditions. An ageing population with increasing health complications signals fiscal pressure and stretched budgets. Those fiscal challenges are more acute, however, because of the violent structures of society that exacerbate and increase ill-health and mental health problems.

The older you are, the more likely you are to live with multiple chronic health conditions, and the more likely you are to being living with dementia. As health is socially determined, it is perhaps no surprise that the poorer you are, the more disadvantaged your circumstances or the more deprived an area you live in, the more likely it is you will suffer from complex and multiple chronic health conditions. Tackling the uneven societal structures that have led to the current crisis of rising multimorbidity and increasing dementia has yet to be seriously engaged with by the government. The executive summary to the 2021 Health and Social Care White Paper, for example, acknowledged the pressures of a larger population that lives longer with more health conditions than before but says nothing of the uneven societal structures which drive this (Department of Health and Social Care, 2021). Given the desire to join up and integrate care around people rather than in institutional silos, their neglect of the wider social, economic and political context for increasing levels of diabetes, obesity, mental health and dementia – all explicitly named – misses the opportunity to address the root cause of the problem of health in society. A study of the ageing population of England, for example, investigated different elements of materialist, psychosocial and behavioural explanations of the social determinants of health on levels of multimorbidity and multiple functional limitations (Singer *et al.* 2019). It found a consistent association with house-hold wealth, sense of control over one's life, physical activity and loneliness. This association extends beyond indicators of social deprivation for individuals alone. As deprivation increases, so does the level of multimorbidity in an area. Dementia is also pat-terned by deprivation. In England and Wales, for example, higher levels of socioeconomic deprivation are associated with increas-ing chances of dying from dementia and dying at a younger age, and higher deprivation can even complicate the quality of your initial diagnosis. In fact, older adults with the least financial resources, an indicator of the level of their socioeconomic depriv-ation, are as much as 50 per cent more likely to develop dementia compared to those with the most money (Cadar *et al.* 2018). Where uneven social structures persist, unequal power will con-tinue to manifest in unequal life chances, with the consequences of unequal power accumulating and worsening as we age. This is perhaps most acute for the ageing ethnic minority population of the UK. The combined effect of persisting social and economic disadvantage with the stressors of racial discrimination means that ethnic minority groups have much poorer health in later life than their white British peers. A decade of fiscal austerity, the eco-nomic consequences of Covid-19 and the impact of stagnating wages unable to match rising living costs will probably see these issues intensify for the last of the baby boomers as they move into older age. Looking to the mechanisms through which unequal power harms health over the life course is particularly important in the context of an ageing population where health and social care is considered a costly and burdensome strain of the national purse strings.

PRECARIOUS LIVES, PRECARIOUS PENSIONS: POOR HEALTH

Living in a crowded, damp house may have immediate consequences for your respiratory or mental health. So might living in a neighbourhood blighted by air pollution. The health and well-being consequences of working in a precarious or demeaning job may also be quickly felt. But the consequences of the low incomes so often bound up with these precarious and disadvantaged lives are also significant in later life. If you are unable to work, you are unable to contribute to a pension plan and, even if you want to, any receipt of means-tested benefits curtails your ability to save for old age. Even those in work may struggle to save for their future given low incomes and rising living costs: "I do think about the future, but there is only so much I can do with the resources I have" (Centre for Ageing Better 2021: 14). It is enough to tackle the precarity of today, let alone plan for the precarity of tomorrow. The state pension scheme was intended to alleviate this financial uncertainty, but despite the triple lock the current state pension is often insufficient on its own, and there is no guarantee of its continued existence for the younger generations of today.

Beveridge saw the state pension as fair reward to those who are past work. It should provide enough to safeguard against want but not so much as to discourage individuals from saving additional funds over their working life. This approach remains, but it is certainly not compatible with means-tested benefits. How can you save for old age if in doing so you reduce your ability to survive today? For Beveridge, as for the policy-makers of today, older people were framed in opposition to the young, working population. Support for older people had to be managed carefully so as not to inflict an "intolerable financial burden on the community" (Beveridge 1942: 92), as this would not be fair according to contemporary political ideas of fairness. But where relative comfort and security in later life – a crucial component to later life health and well-being – depends on the ability to work, buy a home, save and build a pension pot, this entrenches and reproduces sizeable inequalities for older people. Consider again that benefits such as jobseekers' allowance, income support, housing benefit and council tax support are all means tested. Any efforts to save, whether for a rainy day, emergency or your future life, jeopardizes your receipt of those benefits. The people whose health and well-being is most likely to be compromised in later life, those who are most likely to develop multimorbidity, comorbidity or suffer earlier and harder from conditions like dementia, are dependent on benefits earlier in life. Their health is probably already suffering. Insufficient or nonexistent pension in old age amplifies the consequences of a lifetime of accumulated disadvantage. The impact for women will be even more stark: women, who live longer and often in poorer health than men, are also less likely to have secured a sufficient income for their later life. The earning power of women is not equal to that of men. Men are not only paid more for equivalent work but are also more likely to work in occupations and positions deemed worthy of a higher salary. The caring responsibilities overwhelmingly shouldered by women further limits their relative earning potential over their lifetime. The gender gap in pay and earnings is, where pensions are linked to work, simply reproduced in later life.

CARED FOR OR CARE-LESS?

The extent and nature of need in any given population is determined by that population's size, structure and composition: how
many people there are, the number that are female (e.g. what proportion may need gynaecological services), their age and how
are they distributed across the social hierarchy. Since 1942, the
population has grown sizeably and aged significantly. Not only
are we living longer but we are having fewer children. The effect
of this is to shift the age structure of the population upwards.
This matters for healthcare provision and is no small source of
the problems explored in Chapter 6. But the ageing of the population, and the increasing complexity of its needs, throw up bigger
problems than those introduced by a larger population alone.
A growing and ageing population puts pressure on government
purse strings and existing models of public service provision. As
this pressure grows, and so long as neoliberal principles domin-
ate, it is an easy task to see responsibility for old age as falling on
those in old age, particularly during times of economic crisis. The
prevailing political emphasis on the individual is then, although
perhaps unintentionally, shored up by wider policy efforts to
facilitate health promotion in an ageing population. Healthy ageing is aligned to active ageing, with much of the language to date
implicating the individual as the primary agent in achieving it.
Where social and public policy remains imbued with the language
of personal responsibility, this readily negates more meaningful state support and facilitates the continued withdrawal of the
welfare state.

In the last year of life – particularly the last month of life – our
use of healthcare increases markedly, and with it so too do the
costs. In Scotland, for example, one study finds an average cost
of £10,000, with deaths due to cancer associated with the highest number of hospital admissions and dementia accounting for
the least (Diernberger *et al.* 2021). The picture is similar in England

(Luta *et al.* 2020). But in contrast to what you, or indeed the fear-mongers demonizing the costs of an ageing population may think, old age wasn't necessarily associated with either the highest costs or the most frequent hospitalizations. The drivers of high health-care costs in older age are the presence of multiple illnesses and the complexity of end-of-life care, not old age itself. These find-ings offer a useful platform from which to start to unpack some of the erroneous rhetoric surrounding the withdrawal of the welfare state and the burden of older people.

We are, as a society, proud of the NHS. It is a prominent feature of many a general election campaign and, as seen in the 2019 gen-eral election, even managed to overtake concerns around Brexit as the most important issue for adults in Britain (IPSOS Mori 2019). Throughout the height of the Covid-19 pandemic, political messaging sought to leverage this public commitment to the NHS as a means to garner public support for the latest national lockdowns: "Stay Home, Protect the NHS, Save Lives". When faced with spiralling healthcare costs from a population who are, generally, expectant of prevention and cure should illness or accident befall them, raising the spectre of ruinous costs and an overwhelmed NHS to justify changes to welfare provision in the face of an aged and ageing population is all too easy. But if there is robust, empirical evidence to suggest that old age isn't in fact the driver of the highest costs to healthcare, or the most frequent hos-pitalizations overall, where does that leave us? The limitations of our health care system are worsened by its continued discon-nect with the social care system. We may not cost as much to the healthcare budget in our last year of life should we die at the age of 90 rather than say 40, but we have perhaps accumulated a sizeable bill over our lifetime. And depending on the chances that soci-ety affords us, the costs of accumulated exposure to more or less deprived circumstances accrue.

Beveridge confined himself to the provision of clinical and medical care to tackle the giant of Disease, but we, in our holistic understanding of health and well-being, must also consider the provision of social care. The kind of health care provided in the medical environment of a hospital is not the kind of support that most older adults require, which is more about help with bathing, dressing, meals and mobility. To live longer, and perhaps in poorer health, as many of us now will, is less of a burden to those able to live comfortably in older age, to access care and support with limited restriction. As fewer of us marry, and as fewer of us choose to have children, traditional expectations of familial care provision will have to change. Without adequate social care provision that is accessible to all, the pressure to medicalize that care in hospital beds or to neglect older adults' needs entirely will grow. Either way, without planning, the costs (both fiscal and societal) will be much greater.

First, consider that in England older people account for as much as half of the costs of public spending on adult social care, with people aged 65 and over accounting for about two-thirds of local authority-provided care (Age UK 2019). Or that in Northern Ireland people aged 65 and over account for around 40 per cent of the contact with social care (BMA 2020). This is, as you can probably imagine, not likely to meet either all the care needs of those people in receipt of care, let alone all of those who need care. Across the UK, much of adult social care is in the hands of private providers, with the extent of provision subject to typical market conditions. In other words, you get what you pay for. In both contexts, people are increasingly encouraged to plan for and be responsible for their own care. All things being equal, maybe such an approach would be appropriate, even fair, but that is surely only possible if the size and nature of care need was solely the consequence of individual agency and actions in their lifetime.

The experiences of older people through the course of the Covid-19 pandemic are prime examples of the shortcomings of the neoliberal emphasis on the individual. Early government action in response to the threat of Covid-19 was patchy. Older people and the social care system were notable casualties of the prevailing political emphasis on the value of an "economically active" individual and its corresponding ageism. Just before the first national lockdown, imposed on 24 March 2020, people over the age of 70 were encouraged to "shield" by shutting themselves away from loved ones, society and risk. Aside from the dubious implication that an arbitrary age threshold is enough to establish vulnerability, the clear signal was that exposure to Covid-19 was their own responsibility should they not follow such advice. Conspicuously absent was any attention to what this unilateral advice meant for the many older people living alone (how would they buy food?) and for the perennially neglected care home residents and care home staff. What of the mental and physical consequences of isolation and separation from family and loved ones? Perhaps the most damning example of this neglect was the government's refusal to acquiesce to care home provider demands early in the pandemic to test all patients for Covid-19 before discharging them back into their care, or even provide adequate personal protective equipment (PPE). Twenty-five thousand people were discharged from hospitals into care homes in the first month of the pandemic without a Covid-19 test: is it any surprise that 40 per cent of the deaths to Covid-19 in the first wave were to care home residents?

THE PROBLEM OF AGE(ISM)

The ageing of the population is all too readily demonized as a looming cost crisis. It would not be "fair", after all, for the shrinking working population – given our tendency to have fewer children – to shoulder the spiralling costs of the growing aged population. We accept this demonization and argument of intergenerational justice because we have normalized positioning older people in opposition to, and distinct from, younger generations. The language of old age, and the policy responses to it, are couched in terms of dependency, frailty, vulnerability and need. Even the traditional measures used to conceptualize the age structure of the population explicitly refer to "dependency". The "old-age dependency ratio" – a widely used measure – is calculated as the ratio of people aged 65 and over (i.e. state pension age up until April 2021) to the "working-age" population (confusingly refer-ring to those aged 15 to 64). As the size of the "old-age" population increases relative to the size of the "working" population, the burden of the dependency increases. Fewer workers yields lower tax revenues, as well as fewer people working in the sorts of pro-fessions the "dependents" may rely on. The crux of the matter, however, is when does an individual become vulnerable, frail or in some way dependent?

Contrary to what I may have thought, I definitely did not wake up on my eighteenth birthday suddenly a fully fledged adult, wise to the world and completely independent of the care and sup-port of my parents. Why then might I imagine that the morning of attaining state pension age I will suddenly become doddering and infirm? Or that retirement itself should signal incapability and frailty? This is of course somewhat of an embellishment to what social norms really do suggest but not that much. There is an expectation, in some segments of society, that when unem-ployment is high, older workers should step aside and free up jobs for (it can only be assumed) the more productive, more valuable, younger potential workers. In fact the economic downturns of the 1980s saw many a rich country – including the UK – follow just that line of expectation, prioritizing employment schemes for the young and ushering older workers out of the labour market through incapacity benefits and early retirement (Standing 2011). Later, fixed pension ages were introduced, enabling employers to force people to retire regardless of their wishes on reaching the age of 65. Although they have since been abolished, policies like this, and a wider emphasis on the young as opposed to the old, created what has been called the "structured dependency" of the elderly (Townsend 1981). Policies explicitly framed older people as dependent and vulnerable, homogenizing vast sections of the population simply by virtue of their age rather than any change in physical or material circumstances. In dictating or encouraging early retirement, this heralds a loss of work (which so often adds meaning to life) and a probable reduction in income, both of which engineer the social dependency of older people.

The Covid-19 pandemic spawned openly ageist narratives in policy and practice, things that had previously existed but until then gone largely unnoticed. Early responses to the pandemic saw the hashtag #BoomerRemover trending on social media, which was emblematic of the sorts of intergenerational conflict which emerged in our ageist society. Some groups among younger generations felt their lives were unfairly on hold through lockdown simply to protect the lives of those who have already lived. Those arbitrary age thresholds, used to distinguish between who is and who is not vulnerable to Covid-19, thereby informing the unilateral guidance to "shield", were deeply problematic as they drew lines in communities between who was and wasn't safe.

The Covid-19 pandemic betrayed the ageism inherent in society. However, in dismissing older people as a vulnerable, dependent and burdensome group, we hold open the door for our own future relegation from political and public concern. We also then accept as inevitable a possibly avoidable decline in our own physical and mental health. As we age, we go through a continual and reinforcing process of acquiring, expressing and internalizing ageist stereotypes (Carney & Nash 2020). Processes of socialization, beginning in childhood, teach us what is considered socially acceptable and how to interact with members of our community. This can be positive, teaching us how to play with friends and how to share, for example. But through this process, we are also exposed to and then acquire the prevailing stereotypes of older people. In turn, we contribute to the maintenance of those stereotypes. This might be retweeting #BoomerRemover or the seemingly less offensive but more insidious act of buying a humorous birthday card "joking" about the aged female body.

Ageism does work both ways: dismissing the "snowflake" generation and younger voices in decision-making whether in the workplace or wider society is equally damaging. If you accept this intergenerational antagonism, it is worth considering that people with more age-positive attitudes when younger have been found to live as much as 7.5 years longer than those who viewed age more negatively (Levy *et al.* 2002). We internalize the negative stereotypes of an aged, frail person. We then embody those characteristics, accepting our inevitable decline and fragile dependency. In this acceptance, we reinforce the stereotype we have already succumbed to. The impact of this is intensified for those in precarious, disadvantaged circumstances, living in poverty and deprivation. If you are already discriminated against or otherwise marginalized, the consequences of the additional penalty of old age are more severe. Ageism is lethal and, perhaps inevitably, costly. Where we internalize negative stereotypes to the disadvantage of our own health, we amplify the cost of our healthcare in our own on old age. In the United States, for example, researchers estimated that over a single year, ageism can cost as much as $63 billion in healthcare (Levy *et al.* 2020). Given our own high chances of a long life, and the political preoccupation with the possible costs of an aged population, why are we so oblivious to the consequences of this persisting, pernicious prejudice?

Beveridge explicitly framed age as a problem. He saw grappling with the "nature and extent of the provision to be made for old age" as "the most difficult of all the problems of social security" (1942: 90). But age, in and of itself, is not the problem. The problem of old age is this framing of age as a burden rather than everyone being equal partners in society. These issues are compounded when welfare is construed as a means to ensure the economic prosperity of the nation, as Beveridge undeniably saw it, rather than as a goal in and of itself. The "crisis" of expanding lifespans will always, therefore, be framed in competition with the needs of those still considered economically productive. This "crisis" of an aged and ageing population is not because of the fact of its ageing but because of how we tend to define value at an individual and societal level. The crisis is intensified because unequal power leads to unequal life chances as a result of structural violence. We condemn older people as a burden while ensuring the longevity of the very structures that create their dependency and amplify their costs and the burden of disease that they shoulder. The most important and, in some ways, the most difficult of all the problems of social security is not age, it is ageism. In the context of an aged and ageing population, where the sustainability of existing models of welfare and service provision is already under threat, it is time for a shift in perspective.

6

Inequity and inferiority: a dismantled health and social care service

The Spanish flu pandemic of 1918–19 killed 228,000 people in the UK alone. The lack of a universal health service readily able to mobilize nationally, squalid living conditions for many and the diverted attentions of a public and government already plagued by war, created the perfect storm for this emergent flu to flourish. Although war and the infancy of virology are import-ant factors differentiating the experience and response to the pandemic of 1918–19 with the Covid-19 pandemic a hundred years later, there are parallels. The ease with which the Spanish flu spread among the poorer or more crowded segments of soci-ety was, for example, replicated in the more recent pandemic. Covid-19 exacerbated existing inequalities in society, throwing into sharp relief the plight of those living and working in relative disadvantage, precarity and poverty. It also shone a light on the depth of the challenges facing our health and social care system. The history of the Spanish flu of 1918–19 may have been very different were a comprehensive, universal healthcare system already in place. The revolutionary social security system Bev-eridge inspired has been transformative to the health and well-being of the population. But the system developed has not kept pace with the wider transformation of society. Neither Beveridge who imagined it, nor Bevan who implemented it, anticipated an aged and ageing population that is ethnically diverse and that remains persistently unequal. Considering care during the Covid-19 pandemic illuminates the transformations that are now imperative.

CARE IN THE TIME OF COVID-19

Although not without problems, the Covid-19 vaccine rollout is perhaps the best illustration of how and why a universal health-care system can be of instrumental importance in responding to a global health crisis. Under such a system, the vast majority of the population are registered with a single health entity, although this may be administered differently in different geographies. As soon as the vaccine was available, it was relatively straightforward to begin inviting people to receive the vaccination according to a predetermined schedule of priority. In fact, the NHS is practised at this, having championed mass routine vaccination programmes since its inception and through delivery of the annual flu vaccin-ation. The foundations offered by practised vaccine rollouts were undeniably an advantage.

The UK was the first country in the world to grant approval for a Covid-19 vaccine for emergency use in December 2020. Marga-ret Keenan, aged 91, made history as the first recipient of that very vaccine at University Hospital, Coventry. The vaccination pro-gramme demonstrated the NHS at its very best, dependent as it was on the clinical, logistical and management expertise of count-less staff working to protect the population. This rollout saw the recall of retired medics, the training of volunteer vaccinators and the mobilization of an army of community volunteers to marshal patients and support people in the minutes following vaccination. But despite the wins afforded by this mass effort within the NHS, inequalities still emerged tracing well-established fault lines in society and offering the first point from which we can begin to interrogate the pressures on health and social care exposed, and exacerbated, by the Covid-19 pandemic.

THE ADVANTAGES OF WEALTH

Aneurin Bevan, the Labour politician responsible for shepherding in the NHS, famously assured the public that the new healthcare system would no longer see wealth as an advantage nor poverty a disadvantage. It is telling that even amid a crisis such as Covid-19 that aspiration could not be met. As with the Spanish flu, the burden of Covid-19 was shouldered by those living in deprivation or in poorer quality and often overcrowded households, or among people working in occupations that increased their risk of exposure. But despite the widely documented heightened risk to those whose position in life meant their exposure to social determinants of health was more a hazard than an asset, inequalities in coverage and uptake of the vaccine programme quickly emerged. In England, for example, to live in a more deprived area meant you were not only more likely to die from Covid-19, and to die younger than someone in a less deprived area, you were also less likely to have been vaccinated. Although the gap between those who are and are not vaccinated by deprivation does close with age, it does not disappear, as can be seen in Figure 6.1.

RESOURCING INFINITE NEED

Before Beveridge (and the realization of his vision), healthcare was not a right but a luxury. It was doled out via the administrative requirements of the Poor Laws, but it was not the comprehensive sort of treatment we, or indeed the population of 1948, enjoy. Should you fall and break your leg in the UK today, you can go to hospital, have it set, be prescribed painkillers and later, if required, receive physiotherapy for rehabilitation. Should your health deteriorate unexpectedly, you are referred for diagnostics, treatment

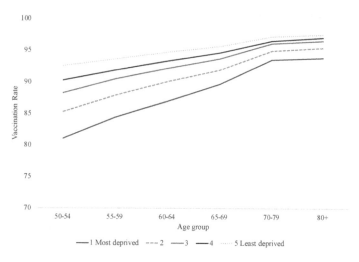

Figure 6.1   Vaccination rates by age and area deprivation,
England, 6 October 2021

Source: OpenSafely (2021).

and, where cure is not possible, palliative care. The UK is excep-
tional in its provision of end-of-life care with an explicit strategy
formalizing the approach. But this is a costly business. As we saw
in Chapter 5, we are at our most expensive in the final year of life
with respect to health and social care. And even the provision of
basic primary care in general practice or community NHS phar-
macies bears a significant price tag. At the heart of much of the
debate that has shadowed the NHS since its inception is working
out how to balance the books: resourcing infinite need with finite
resources. At the population level, this means decisions have to
be made about what is financed and what is not. But the administration of the NHS is devolved across the constituent countries
of the UK and within its different regions. This means that some
decisions about what is financed and what is not are taken at
the subnational level, leading to variations in the exact nature of

health and social care available across the UK. This contributes to the often-cited "postcode lottery" to healthcare, with variations in anything from the type of drugs prescribed for different conditions to the nature (and wait time) for different therapeutic or surgical interventions.

Variations in waiting times and the types of treatment available, however, are perhaps inevitable in a national service caring for a highly diverse population. If you happen to live in a place where there are more people towards the end of their life, the nature of waiting times for some medical or surgical interventions may well be longer compared to those in an area with a relatively youthful population. Following the same logic, it is no surprise that in the face of a rapidly spreading virus to which some groups of the population are more vulnerable than others, shortages and variations in care experience arise. However, uneven and unprecedented demand were not the sole reasons behind the shortages that began to emerge through the course of the pandemic. In fact, the pressures of Covid-19 simply exposed structural holes in the management of the NHS, in terms of both supply and the infrastructure it operates within. PPE is the first line of defence for all health and social care professionals working at the coalface of the pandemic. Very quickly, in early 2020, stocks began to deplete. The scale of the pandemic was unprecedented, as was the scale of resources it consumed. But in England and Wales, for example, the NHS procurement system should have been able to cope. Two years earlier, the Department of Health and Social Care set up "NHS Supply Chain", which was tasked with developing and maintaining the infrastructure to resource NHS trusts. Their inability to manage the pressure of Covid-19 and effectively scale up their existing procurement agreements saw local NHS trusts taking matters into their own hands, with different levels of success, driving up competition for the already scarce supplies of PPE and leading to inequalities of access (Sanchez-Graells 2020a).

Although the public was urged not to buy stocks of surgical-grade face masks – the sort of masks that homecare providers depend on – poignant images began to surface of health and social care workers crafting PPE out of bin liners and duct tape. Respiratory masks that were delivered to hospitals and general practices were, according to an anonymous whistle-blower reported in the BBC, relabelled with new, unexpired expiry dates (Press 2020). Public Health England reassurances that the masks had been rigorously safety tested did not dispel unease. Alongside questionable facemasks, one of the most attention-grabbing headlines surrounding the PPE scandal was the incomplete, late and ultimate delivery of faulty gowns collected by the RAF from a supplier in Turkey (Rawlinson 2020). Although countries worldwide were competing for dwindling supplies, the failure of existing structures within the NHS were not the only problem. A not insignificant sum of £18 billion was spent on contracts awarded in the first months of the pandemic, but the procurement procedures used can best be described as improper and at worst downright corrupt. Back-channel lines of communications saw those who were chummy with MPs and cabinet members – so-called VIPs – gaining access to highly lucrative contracts involving more than just PPE (Dyer 2022). Despite being costly, you might at least hope that the outcomes of the contracts would be effective, but this was certainly not a given.

What was a scandal in a crisis reveals structural weaknesses in the existing procurement and supply chain systems of the NHS in England that predated the pandemic. Albert Sanchez-Graells persuasively attributes this fiasco to the institutional uncertainty induced by continuous cycles of reform and reshuffle within the NHS and the consequences of a decade of fiscal austerity (2020b). Resourcing infinite need is impossible at the best of times, but if it is not attempted through properly regulated systems supported by sound infrastructure then inequalities are inevitable. Uneven power dynamics and questionable politicking brought the NHS to the brink even before it sought to care for a population in crisis. The consequences of this were then disproportionately borne by those least able to bear it, and that extends to the NHS staff already on their knees.

HONOUR THY PHYSICIAN

Ten days into the first UK national lockdown, streets up and down the country erupted into cheers and applause to "clap for carers", an opportunity to stand in solidarity with those putting their lives on the line. But as more and more government politicians were pictured clapping and cheering, their stance in solidarity could not have seemed more contrived. Inadequate PPE and provisions were just the tip of the iceberg in terms of the strain endured by health and social care staff. Pre-pandemic, staffing shortages across the NHS were commonplace. Indeed, staff shortages in the nursing profession are as well established as the NHS itself. Going into the Covid-19 pandemic, estimates suggested a shortfall of 40,000 nurses: not far off the initial shortage of 48,000 nurses at the inception of the NHS (Charlesworth 2021).

But the 70 years that have passed should have taught those responsible for the NHS the importance of adequate investment in training and proper regard for the supply of staff. For example, as public purse strings tightened in the wake of the global financial crisis of 2008, the nurse training budget became a ready target. Yet warnings from health leaders and universities abounded, urging caution given the likelihood of an increased demographically driven demand for nurses in the future. The government steamed ahead regardless. By 2018 the UK had only 30.9 nurse graduates per 100,000 population, performing relatively poorly compared to many of other Organisation for Economic Co-operation and Development countries such as Australia (109), Switzerland (108) and even the United States (66) (OECD n.d). Underinvestment in medical training creates gaps that can only be filled at times of crisis or shortage by overseas recruitment. But a reliance on overseas recruitment is not compatible with current political efforts to establish and maintain a hostile environment for immigrants while also encouraging rhetoric tending to dismiss "foreign" workers as costly, unskilled and consumers of domestic resources. The toxicity of Brexit did nothing to alleviate these issues, with stories circulating of NHS EU nationals leaving as the UK exited the EU.

Whereas nurses have perhaps been chronically underfunded, doctors and surgeons have enjoyed relative security. But nurses, doctors and surgeons have all fared better than healthcare assistants, care workers, porters and cleaners. The hierarchical structures of society are as apparent within healthcare as they are in society at large. The chasm between those at the top (our doctors and surgeons) versus those at the bottom (our cleaners, porters and care assistants) became acutely visible through the course of the pandemic. The NHS could not function without cleaners, porters and the whole gamut of auxiliary staff who keep patients and staff moving, clean, fed and secure. But these groups are often poorly paid, poorly treated and poorly protected. They, and nurses, are also more likely to be employed on insecure contracts. The precarity inherent to insecure agency work and zero-hour contracts was compounded by the uncertainties of the pandemic. The consequences of underfunding health and social care, while undervaluing particular occupations within the care sector, are severe. Not only does it limit individual ability to provide high-quality care, as evidenced by previous warnings from the Royal College of Midwives of an exodus of midwifery staff (2021), it undermines public confidence and trust in a system where people at the limits of their capacity to cope and care become the focal point for public anger at neglect and failed treatment. We misdirect frustration and demands for action when we only condemn a failing NHS hospital or struggling care home. Although it is imperative to address failings within a care provider, this is simply a symptom of the root problem: chronic underfunding, mismanagement and politicking seeking to jettison responsibility for health and social care.

Nowhere are the tensions between provision of high-quality care and underfunding more apparent than in our adult social care system. Today, our population is more ethnically diverse, we are living longer, we are more likely to survive traumatic and early birth and we are exposed to an ever more complicated set of influences on our health and well-being. The basic tenet of Beveridge's vision for tackling the giant of Disease – which became the NHS – was premised on a biomedical model of health favouring the silver bullet of medical and, increasingly, pharmaceutical intervention. The goal was to return a body in the deviant state of *ill-health* or *dis-ease* to wellness to ensure that all men are able to continue contributing to a prosperous and growing economy while all women are well positioned to raise a nation. Such a view, no matter how radical and revolutionary, did not leave space for the wider provision of social care to maintain individual and population well-being and health. Nor was it perhaps as essential back then. Today, our care needs may have become more complex. For those who have lived a life of relative disadvantage, in their older age they are contending with the adversity of the cumulated exposure to hazardous social determinants of health that the more advantaged among are not. We do not, however, account for that in our system of care.

Funding of state-provided social care is woefully inadequate and was decimated by the decade of fiscal austerity following the global financial crisis. Covid-19 simply made a chronic problem acute. Even before the austerity drive, efforts to reduce spiralling costs across health and social care saw a change in the nature of the service provision. One social care worker wrote, in a letter to the *Guardian*, of their dismay at the change from supporting those in difficulty to only those considered in danger (Robertson-Molloy 2021). People working with children and adults who have special educational needs have seen their budgets, and therefore capacity, slashed dramatically. And care home workers are, by all accounts, at the bottom of priorities and budget lines. The amount of care we can therefore expect to receive is dependent on the amount our local authority can afford to provide and the amount we can afford to contribute individually on top of that. This is true across our lifespan, whether we have care needs associated with living with a disability or care needs that arise as we age or become ill. The provision and receipt of care is also shaped by the context of our private lives. Some of us will care for our ailing parents and grandparents while also looking after our own children. This can take its toll: "Caring for my parents was very hard, I was happy to do it, but it was just tough. You never seem to stop . . . it's hard with children . . . you half-do everything" (Centre for Ageing Better 2021: 20).

Pushing responsibility for care into the realms of our private lives feeds inequality. The health of people with caring responsibilities suffers, and the degree of care for people in need varies according to their and their family members' time, resources and flexibility to manage care alongside their own lives (Centre for Ageing Better 2021). The neglect of care workers – across all types of need – is criminally short-sighted. Care assistant roles, by and large, are low paid, often temporary and with minimal or no formal qualifications required. The job is undervalued and considered routine and low-skilled, and its importance to those cared for is rarely acknowledged. If we do not train our care workers, we dismiss as marginal the significance of our care needs and ignore the uneven burden of responsibility placed on individuals and families. For successive governments since the creation of the NHS, and of course the gradual expansion of the provision of social care, the question of how much to provide with increasingly stretched resources has proved intractable. Our care needs are infinite but the resources are finite.

SUPPLYING FINITE CARE

If a person dies of tuberculosis today who could otherwise have been cured, we should, as argued in Chapter 1, construe this as violence. But it is not that simple. Despite all the medical resources available, they are not at the disposal of everyone in the world. Health and social care is a costly business that is made more costly as the complexity of need in a population increases. Even the wealth of high-income countries is not sufficient to grant access to all the medical resources available to everyone. But consider the difference in expenditure on healthcare between the United States and the UK. In the UK, we spend around 10 per cent of our gross domestic product (GDP) on healthcare, and have done since 2009 after a concerted spending increase under Blair's Labour administration. We could spend some time asking why that expenditure has remained the same, despite an aged and age-ing population with increasing and more complex care needs. But rather than delve into an economic debate, let's consider exactly how a fixed budget for health and social care is shared out and what the implications of those decisions are.

In contrast to the UK, the USA spends as much as 16 per cent of its GDP on healthcare in a system that is not univer-sal and, across a range of measures, results in poorer health outcomes than we see in the UK. Greater expenditure does not equate to better care, it seems. The relative success of the UK's model lies in its approach to rationing. Rationing is a dirty word in the context of health and social care. No one wants to think that one lifesaving or life-transforming drug or treatment is not available to them because of rationing. And yet no system of health or social care can expect to meet the infinite care needs of the population it serves. Decisions must be made as to what can be bought and who can receive it. For much of the UK, for example, decisions on medical care and, since April 2013, social care, are informed by the National Institute for Care Excellence

(NICE),[1] established in 1999. NICE make their recommendations according to an assessment of how many years in good health a particular therapeutic or medical intervention will bring. Despite national guidance, local variation can emerge, particularly where funding granted to different health administrative geographies (e.g. Clinical Commissioning Groups in England or Local Health Boards in Wales) varies. GPs, in their capacity as gatekeepers to wider health and social care, play a key role in the rationing process. For every patient they refer, every drug they prescribe, that is one portion of their fixed budget spent.

So what are the consequences of this approach to rationing? On the one hand it has, since 1948, ensured that a fairly comprehensive system of health and, more recently, social care is available to the population when they need it. Yet on the other, as evidenced by Covid-19, the rationing approach allows room for morally questionable decisions over the provision of care, the devaluing of life and the explosion of inequalities in access to timely, lifesaving diagnostics and treatment. An acute example of this was the controversy around the use of "do-not-resuscitate" (DNR) orders to inform decisions on the provision of lifesaving treatment for Covid-19 patients. DNRs were reportedly applied to people according to age and the presence of a learning disability in otherwise healthy individuals, stating that if these people contracted Covid-19 they would not be resuscitated should their breathing or heart stop. This extended beyond the first wave of Covid-19 despite a damning report from the Care Quality Commission (2020) stating that the use of DNRs had led to potentially avoidable deaths. Decisions made on an objective calculation of how many years of good health an intervention may bring do not allow for sensitivity to the breadth of life that we should value in

---

1   NICE guidance covers England, Wales and Northern Ireland. Scotland is coved by SIGN, an organization that develops and disseminates national clinical guidelines including guidance from NICE.

society. To be old is not to be expendable. To live with a learning disability is not to live needlessly. The underlying message that some lives were worth less than those of others created space for careless remarks like "they would have died soon anyway", as numbers of deaths to older people and those with learning disabilities soared. It also saw a prevalent narrative dismissing the deaths of those with underlying health problems as inevitable and therefore somehow less meaningful. This devaluation of life is morally questionable at the very least, but the assumption that "they would have died soon anyway" is also wrong. Between March 2020 and March 2021, 1.5 million potential years of life were lost to Covid-19 in the UK, with estimates suggesting that for each of the 146,000 people who died they lost an average of just over a decade of life (Krelle & Tallack 2021).

Any casual conversation about the state of the care sector in the UK probably revolves around two key concerns: how easy it is to get an appointment with your GP and hospital waiting times. GPs are the workhorses of the NHS and the first point of contact for most patients. As primary care providers, they are generalists spanning health promotion, prevention and rehabilitation, as well as the referral point for specialist secondary care. What they are not is superhuman, nor are there enough of them. Just as the UK performs poorly in terms of the number of nurse graduates per 100,000 population, we perform similarly poorly on number of doctors per person. More worrying, since 2014 the number of GPs trained, recruited and practising has not kept pace with the size of the population. Analysis from the Nuffield Trust suggests that England, Wales and Scotland all saw a decline in the number of GPs per 100,000 population since around 2009, although numbers have generally increased steadily in Northern Ireland since the late 1970s (Palmer 2019). It is inevitable that demand will outpace supply when gaps appear between the number of GPs relative to the size of the population, particularly in an aged and ageing population. This was true before the pandemic and even

more so through the course of it. Not only was general practice
dealing with the unprecedented demand of Covid-19, but GPs
were also trying to continue meeting the wider health needs of
their patients within the varying constraints of social distancing,
human resourcing challenges and supply issues. It is inevitable
that this level of pressure would challenge general practice's
ability to ensure that everyone who seeks an appointment can
get one. But it is a challenge that greater sensitivity to the wider
pressures already building within primary care pre-pandemic, a
more concerted attempt to recruit medical students into general
practice and greater investment in training to support increased
numbers could have lessened.

Circling out from primary care, the crisis illuminated by the
pandemic deepens. Hospital waiting times have long tormented
governments trying to manage supply and demand within health
and social care. But they were not an immediate consequence of
the UK approach to rationing. It was not until 1951 that successive
annual reports into the provision of care began to talk of waiting
lists (Appleby & Thorlby 2008). Nevertheless, waiting lists and
waiting times have since featured prominently and persistently
in public and political debate. Where wait times are lengthy, some
of us can afford to go private, or enjoy the perks of a health insurance policy with their job. There is an argument that suggests
clinicians who practise both privately and publicly are unlikely to
try and reduce waiting lists as this would impact lucrative private
practice. But regardless, the option to go private is not open to all.
Waiting lists can therefore indirectly widen health inequalities in
the population as some are forced to endure the wait while others
can afford the alternative. Where waits vary between regions, inequalities can become even more entrenched. There is, though,
a hierarchy to wait times, whether for diagnostics or treatment.
The pain of a delayed hip replacement is no doubt unspeakable,
but the consequences of a delayed cancer diagnosis can be fatal.

REFORMING HEALTH AND SOCIAL CARE

In 2010, the newly elected Conservative–Liberal Democrat coalition published their long-term vision for the NHS titled "Equity and Excellence: Liberating the NHS". The vision set out seemed to entrench a biomedical model of health, annexing public health from the remit of the NHS and thereby appearing to give primacy to treatment of ill-health rather than either the prevention or promotion of good health. Publicized as striving to build a "patient-centred" NHS, the reforms this White Paper ushered in have much to answer for in consolidating the crisis unfolding in providing for the health and well-being of the population. Rather than the equity and excellence it sought to promote, it continued the dismantling of the NHS that Beveridge envisaged so that inequity and inferiority are perhaps more apt descriptors. Here, however, we are not dissecting the failings of those reforms nor the failings of the many that have come before. It is sufficient to recognize that a process of sustained reorganization, the continual introduction of new and ever more difficult metrics and the consolidation of market-based conditions as the basis for the provision of healthcare challenge the sustainability of the NHS and the willpower of its workforce. A bigger challenge, however, is the continued disconnect between the provision of health and social care. An integrated system of health and social care would, in an ideal world, place the patient and their needs at the centre of an interconnected web of service provision. Barriers within and between health and social care would be broken down, with different specialities maintaining their siloed expertise without undermining a holistic approach to the provision of care and decision-making. Such an integrated system would stand up to the contemporary giant of Disease. This giant is not something to be slayed with a silver bullet of medical, surgical or pharmaceutical intervention alone. The root cause of many of these ills requires the reconfiguration of society through which structural violence is wrought. But there are also elements of this structural violence that can be readily tackled. Targeted investment in areas of deprivation, for example, beyond the grey infrastructure of transport systems and roads. Schemes that foster and enhance community engagement and resilience or attention to the social infrastructure required. But the social thinking required goes beyond thinking on the social, environmental or political determinants of health alone. So too must it call into question the prevailing dominance of biomedical models of health that either naïvely neglect or wilfully ignore broader understandings of what it is to be healthy and what is needed to ensure that. This is all too apparent in the marginalization of minority ethnic groups with different cultural backgrounds and perceptions of appropriate health and social care in our approach to the provision of care. The Covid-19 vaccine rollout is but one example of why it is imperative to think on the different characteristics of the population served by the NHS. Ensuring the provision of culturally sensitive services has to go further than the vaccine rollout. For example, counselling and mental health support services need more than the offer of an interpreter to ensure they have meaning for all in our population.

Reforming health and social care is no small task, but we need to do more than simply reform the current system. This system is no longer sustainable, with neither the resources nor the capability to address the increasingly complex health and well-being needs of a larger, more diverse and older population. Ready access to our beloved NHS has come at a price. We expect what ails us to be easily cured, too often demanding receipt of a prescription for antibiotics to cure the common cold, the chesty cough and more. But this reliance on the perceived quick fix of a pill has contributed to the growing threat and indeed reality of antibiotic resistance, as we will see in Chapter 7. Beveridge's blueprint for the NHS heralded significant improvements to the life chances and well-being of the population. Access to universal health care complemented the wider changes to housing, education, work and safeguarding against poverty. But it has perhaps been a victim of its own success, with the capability to do more and more for the health of the population simultaneously eroding its capacity to do so. At the same time, as the costs of providing for such a comprehensive service increase, themselves amplified by the consequences of our unequal society, budgets have been stretched or cut and the workforce pushed to breaking point. Radical reform is needed to combat both the emerging crises and continuing challenges faced.

7

Continuing challenges, contemporary crises

Nicholas Timmins, biographer of the welfare state, reflected that it was not only Beveridge's proposals that were remarkable, but also their enduring resonance with the parameters of political and public debate on the welfare state today (Timmins 2017). The thorny issue of how best to manage housing benefits in a country of vast geographical inequalities in housing costs; the difficulties defining poverty; the fair and equal treatment of women; and the significant challenges reconciling a rights-based system with sufficient benefits to sustain a healthy standard of living without disincentivizing either work or saving. Have any of these challenges been satisfactorily addressed? An eye to the violence of a decade of austerity and the crisis of Covid-19 suggests not. Both eroded hard-won gains for equality, not just in gender but across many protected characteristics. Where the burden of care disproportionately falls on women, women will always be more vulnerable to cuts in welfare and social security. Women will also be more vulnerable to the consequences of a global health crisis where care needs increase both in the public and private realm. Finally, both fiscal austerity and Covid-19 showed with painful clarity the consequences of underinvestment and disinvestment in the health and social care workforce. Beveridge wanted to secure "improved labour standards, economic advancement, and social security" for all (1942: 171). And he did, to a point. But the emerging inequalities first evidenced in the Black Report, the political squabbling over what is fair and the continued refusal to face up to the consequences of uneven power for uneven life chances have made a renewal of Beveridge's survey of the five giants more critical than ever. But where should our attention now be focused?

The early deaths of our children, the causes and consequences of their increasing weight and the mental health epidemic are clear alarm bells. There is an obvious need to dismantle the structures that not only disadvantage people over their lifetime but make them less able to manage the consequences of a lifetime of disadvantage in increasing old age. We are living longer but often in poorer health. The problem of age(ism) has made that only too clear. But these are not the only challenges facing society, nor do they capture the extent of emerging crises that will threaten health and well-being for decades to come. Let us first pick up the thread of austerity that has ran throughout this book, before turning to the emerging crises wrought by the success of societal advancement.

THE VIOLENCE OF AUSTERITY

One of the greatest markers of success in modern society is perhaps the sustained improvements to life expectancy so many of us have enjoyed over the last century. Recall the babies born in the shadow of Beveridge's vision. In 1942, although they could have expected to live to around 60, by their sixtieth birthday they were looking to enjoy another 20 years or so of life. The advances in later ages are mirrored by the hard-won reductions to mortality in the first days, months and years of life. But we became complacent, assuming the gains to life expectancy were both irreversible and universal in one of the richest countries in the world with a comprehensive and free universal health care service. How wrong we were. The social determinants of health, wielding their influence through material, psychosocial and behavioural pathways, among others, mean some are more likely to live longer and in better health than others. Your chances of a long and healthy life depend on where you are born and who you are born to. The enduring influence of the context of your birth on your later life can be seen in the places you school, the jobs you do or do not get and the social networks you move in. This is perhaps most visible through where you live.

We saw in Chapter 3 how chances of a long life vary across the country, and this sort of variation remains true as we age, as shown in Figures 7.1 and 7.2. These maps compare life expectancy at 65 for males and females across areas of the UK, relative to the average life expectancy in the UK for males and females, respectively. Each area is shaded according to whether the time left to live is greater or lower than the UK average.

The scale of these inequalities in life expectancy is even more stark when we look within areas of the UK rather than only at the regional or country level. But the injustice intensifies when we consider differences in just how many years of life we can expect to live in good health. Across the UK, the biggest gap in healthy life expectancy is contained within a mere 15-mile radius: women aged 65 in Newham, London have only 5.2 years of good health ahead of them compared to 16.7 years for women in Brent. What can you do with more than a decade of life in good health? What difference will it make to how much you can earn or save? How much more of your life will you spend independently? Within Scotland, the gap in healthy life expectancy stands at 8.02 years for women, but over a distance of 300 miles rather than only 15. For women in Falkirk, those with the fewest years ahead in good health, this accounts for only 42 per cent of their years left to live. Not only do women living in the Orkney Islands live much longer, but nearly 78 per cent of those years are in good health. The costs

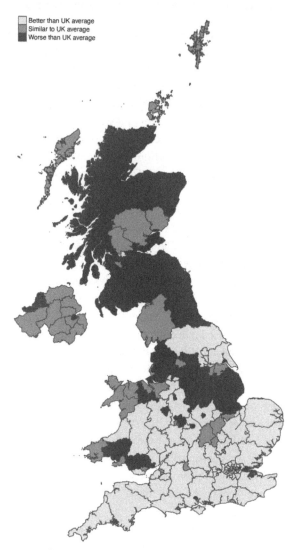

Figure 7.1 Life expectancy at age 65, compared to UK average, women, 2017–19

Source: Office for National Statistics (2021c).

Note: Isles of Scilly and City of London are excluded, as figures are not calculated for these areas because of small numbers of deaths and populations.

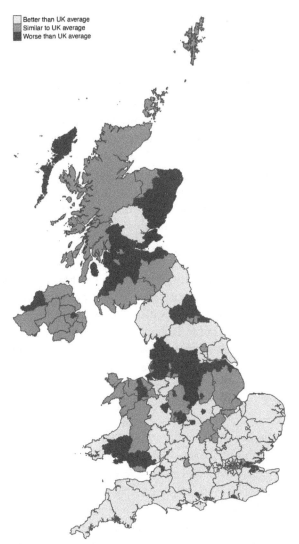

Figure 7.2 Life expectancy at age 65, compared to UK average, men, 2017–19

Source: Office for National Statistics (2021c).

Note: Isles of Scilly and City of London are excluded, as figures are not calculated for these areas because of small numbers of deaths and populations.

of those years, to the state, to the community or family and to
the individual are wildly different. A similar picture exists both
for men and across Wales and Northern Ireland. We have reaped
the rewards of Beveridge's investment into our health, our living
situation, our work and our education. But we do so unevenly,
and the provisions he made have not been sufficient to combat
the widening social gaps in society nor their harmful relationship with health outcomes. Although we are living longer, the
toll of living longer but often in poorer health is heavy. For those
in their later years, this toll interacts with and is compounded by
prevailing attitudes towards older people, those attitudes we internalize and embody, further compromising our own physical and
mental well-being.

Where you live can kill you. So said Clare Bambra back in 2016
as she documented the health divides in our nation. But today,
where you live, and who you are, kills more quickly than it once
did. After a century of improvements to life expectancy, the rate
of improvement began to falter. The Department of Health and
Social Care was quick to dismiss early alarm bells rung by the
likes of Lu Hiam, Danny Dorling and Martin McKee as a product
of their personal bias rather than statistical insight (Hiam *et al*.
2018). And yet, the evidence began to mount. Critics of the alarm
that was starting to ripple through some areas of the public health
community pointed to similar stalls in life expectancy elsewhere,
including the United States, or argued that there are obvious limits to life expectancy. We can't live forever, so at some point the
rate of improvement has to plateau. That is all well and good, but
why did we begin to plateau before other countries? For example,
women in countries as disparate as France, Germany, Greece, Ireland, Norway, Spain and Sweden will all live longer than women
in the UK. And the stalling and ultimate plateauing of life expectancy as inevitable is only a defensible argument if it applies to all.
Yet the stalling of improvements to life expectancy were not only
uneven within the population, building on existing inequalities

in life expectancy; for some life expectancy actually began to fall. Women in the most deprived areas of England suffered first, but the onslaught of a global health crisis saw the situation worsen. Life expectancy for men in England fell in 2020 for the first time in 40 years by an average of 1.3 years. Women too saw wider falls no longer restricted to those living in the most deprived areas, losing 0.9 years to their life expectancy (Public Health England 2021). But it was those living in the most deprived areas who suffered the greatest loss. According to Public Health England, not only had life expectancy reached its lowest levels since 2011 in September 2021, inequalities in life expectancy by deprivation were also at their widest for all previous years for which they had data (since around the turn of the millennium) (Public Health England 2021). The gap between the most and least deprived areas was 10.3 years for men and 8.3 years for women. The loss to years of life through Covid-19 was not simply to people "who would have died anyway" and were already approaching their final months: 146,000 people lost an average of just over a decade of life, which amounts to 1.5 million years of life gone to Covid-19 (Krelle & Tallack 2021). Even before the devastation of Covid-19, the faltering to life expectancy meant that as many as a million years of potential life would be lost in the UK by 2058. Almost all of those years expected to be lost are to people in their forties and fifties today (Dorling 2017).

Efforts to dismiss concern on faltering and falling life expectancy expanded beyond differences in political rhetoric. The role of cold winters and the flu was attributed as the cause of the rise in deaths among older people (Office for National Statistics 2018). Others suggested that previous improvements to interventions in cardiovascular disease had run their course (Raleigh 2018). All these points will have played a role, but it is the violence of austerity that we should interrogate. By 2020, the weight of voices attributing falling life expectancy to the consequences of austerity were hard to ignore. Most notably, perhaps, the preamble to the updated landmark Marmot Review was damning about a decade of failings that saw the situation worsen beyond the inequalities previously reported back in 2010:

> From rising child poverty and the closure of children's centres, to declines in education funding, an increase in precarious work and zero hours contracts, to a housing affordability crisis and a rise in homelessness, to people with insufficient money to lead a healthy life and resorting to food banks in large numbers, to ignored communities with poor conditions and little reason for hope ... Austerity will cast a long shadow over the lives of the children born and growing up under its effects. (Marmot *et al*. 2020: 5)

Recognition of both the social production of health and the reality of unequal power structures contributing to unequal life chances means it is difficult to ignore the consequences of fiscal austerity to our health and well-being. Austerity systematically dismantled the support and infrastructure able to bolster disadvantaged communities, deprived places and poor people. Incidences of the violent consequences of austerity are readily identifiable. Between 2010 and 2014, for example, more than 45,000 additional people died because of the severity of cuts to health and social care spending, leading to calls for improved delivery of social care and the training and recruitment of more nurses. The later dramatic rise in deaths to some of the oldest and frailest of our population in 2015 was linked to delays in discharging patients from hospital and explained by stretched and strained social care services (Green *et al*. 2017b). The spike in old-age mortality seen in 2015 was truly remarkable, reflecting one of the biggest annual increases in mortality since the Second World War (Green *et al*. 2017a). Alongside wider reductions to spending on social care, changes in income support for poorer pensioners contributed to this increase, all of which are a product of austerity

(Loopstra *et al.* 2016). However, it is not by any means only older people or those in hospital who suffer the consequences of fiscal austerity. The link between entitlement to benefit support and active pursuit of work, after its introduction under Labour, intensified under fiscal austerity (see Chapter 5). "Fairness" was used to justify tightening benefits criteria to protect the taxes of hardworking individuals from the lazy benefit scroungers. But the demonization of the so-called "benefit scrounger" is more insidious when applied to disabled people dependent on benefits to live in a stubbornly ableist society.

To live with a disability is to live with additional "inescapable costs" to the ones we all otherwise carry. On top of your mortgage or rent, you must also manage the costs of things like a wheelchair and perhaps the additional bedroom needed for a care worker. Those costs are magnified where society remains modelled on an "able" body whose value is their economic productivity. Yet it was not until 2018 that a meaningful metric accounting for the hidden costs of disability were incorporated into estimates of UK poverty: this concluded that as many as half of the families living in poverty included a disabled person (Social Metrics Commission 2018). Frances Ryan's (2019) damning account of the impact of austerity on disabled people is a hard read that illuminates the continued abuse and neglect of disabled people in society. Entering into a global pandemic, in which people with underlying health conditions were already more vulnerable, disabled people had already suffered more under austerity, a situation that was exacerbated by their increasing demonization as scrounging, lazy liars. At its extremes, Ryan argued, the large-scale negligence of disabled people was tantamount to abuse. We should, I think, go further than that. Abuse and violence capture more than the extremes, as the abandonment of disabled people through the course of the pandemic made only too clear. Austerity is, through Galtung's concept of structural violence, violent. It perpetuates unequal power by limiting opportunities for support to those who

need it most. This manifests in unequal life chances and, according to Chris Grover (2019), is far more than just abuse, it is social
murder.

In 2017, Jodey Whiting had been hospitalized for a brain cyst.
She was also suffering from pneumonia. This bout of illness, on
top of wider mental health problems and the pressures of being
a mother to nine children, meant she missed a letter calling her
to a fit-to-work test from the Department of Work and Pensions (DWP). Means-tested benefits are violently enforced in
our shrinking welfare state and the DWP refused to believe that
Jodey's missed appointment was because of ill-health: she was
deemed in breach of her benefit conditions. Her employment
support allowance, housing benefit and council tax benefit were
all stopped. Jodey took her own life six days later. Jodey's story is
one of many, including one of three equally appalling examples
of our catastrophically failing system reported in a *Guardian* art-
icle in the Spring of 2020 (Butler 2020). The real people in these
stories give meaning to statistics finding an additional six suicides for every 10,000 work capability assessments, for example.
If you cut financial lifelines, you force people to choose between
heating their homes and feeding themselves or their family. You
increase the risk of malnutrition in childhood and the likelihood
of depression, anxiety and low well-being. If you remove support
services, you leave people bereft and abandoned, increasing the
risk of social isolation and loneliness. The violent consequences
of austerity to our health because of the impact on poverty and
the environments in which we live are unequivocal. Austerity's
long shadow will harm the health and well-being of the children of today far into their adulthood. The long-term economic
costs, both in the consequences for health and social care and
the impact on the earning potential of these children, will be sizeable. But austerity is not the only challenge our welfare state must
contend with.

CLIMATE CHANGE

New Year's Day 2022 was the warmest on record for the UK. Many in the mainstream media cheerily commented on this, welcoming the balmy temperatures as a contrast to the cold and rain once so typical of the mid-winter season. Yet the mild winter days alongside the searing temperatures increasingly reached in the summer months should raise alarm rather than spirits. Political inaction against the threat of climate change and the glorification of uncharacteristically warm weather might suggest indifference in public opinion to the consequences of our warming world. And yet, polling from the Health Foundation published in October 2021 suggests that four in five people view climate change as a global emergency (Cameron *et al*. 2021). How can it be anything but a global emergency when the WHO suggests that between 2030 and 2050, climate change will be responsible for an additional 250,000 deaths per year? Not only do people recognize that climate change poses a major threat to people's health globally (86 per cent), just under three-quarters of people polled by the Health Foundation also agreed that climate change threatens people's health in the UK. Where once climate change was pleasantly equated with warmer summer days, the threat to life and livelihoods is, by the public at least, increasingly accepted. What, then, are the consequences of climate change for health and well-being in the UK?

In the summer of 2020, there were 2,556 excess deaths (excluding deaths from Covid-19) during periods of unusual heat (Oliver 2021). However, despite the apparent acceptance of the relationship between climate change and health, people don't tend to consider themselves as vulnerable to heat in the UK. Nevertheless, by 2050 the number of heat-related deaths is expected to triple, with the temperatures from the hottest summers on record becoming the norm. When you are too hot, your body sweats to cool you down. But if you sweat too much, the dehydration can prove fatal. High temperatures can also lead to heat stroke and heat exhaustion, both of which can also lead to death. Older people living in care homes, and older people living alone, are most at risk of heat-related mortality. There is also evidence to suggest, internationally at least, that people from lower socioeconomic groups are also more vulnerable. Poorer-quality homes and the costs associated with air-conditioning systems or even simply running a fan go some way in explaining this differing vulnerability.

Yet the threat to human health from rising temperatures in the UK goes beyond just the ability of the body to keep cool. Globally, people are well versed with the risk heralded by a mosquito bite. In Africa, for example, as of 2019 there were around 170.9 million cases of malaria reported, a disease transmitted through mosquito bites (Statista 2021). In the UK, there are already established mosquito populations able to transmit malaria and, it is assumed, other pathogens to people (Baylis 2017). As temperatures continue to rise, non-native mosquitoes may also be able to reach UK shores, bringing with them diseases such as West Nile virus, dengue fever and Zika virus. The consequences of these zoonotic diseases – diseases which have made the jump from animals to humans – have been made all too clear through the global spread and destruction of Covid-19. And yet, for some the threat of emerging vector-borne diseases may seem a vague and "foreign" prospect, abstracted from the consequences of climate change.

As temperatures rise, not only will the UK be likely to see hotter and drier summers but also warmer and wetter winters. At the same time, the frequency and intensity of extreme weather events is likely to increase, with devastating consequences. In England, for example, deaths from flooding were at a record high in 2019–20, a trend that is likely to continue. But even when lives are not lost, the trauma of losing one's home or business to a flood is significant. "It was terrifying . . . the furniture is wet . . . It's devastation", despaired Lilias Ahmeira after the flash flooding which destroyed homes in Somerset in June 2021 (BBC News 2021). "I looked through the letterbox and it was like looking out to sea ... my house was full of water", remembered Keri Muldoon, whose house was one of the many ravaged by the River Irwell in December 2015 (Mwamba 2021). The burden of climate change evidently extends beyond physical ill-health or mortality. Indeed, anxiety, depression and post-traumatic stress disorder are all associated with the trauma of experiencing a flood.

Extreme weather can kill, injure or take its toll on mental health and well-being. But the consequences of climate change to health are seen in more than heat and rain. From the industrial revolution onwards, technological advances heralded gains in health and longevity. At the same time, however, those advances were coupled with a shift towards ever more resource-intensive lifestyles around the world, particularly in the Global North. As we produce and consume at unprecedented levels, we contribute to air pollution and global warming, the harbinger of climate change. As many as 40,000 excess deaths a year in the UK are already attributed to air pollution, costing the UK economy more than £20 billion annually (Royal College of Physicians 2016). Although public opinion is conscious of the consequences of climate change for health, as noted above, there is still entrenched resistance to any efforts to mitigate the consequences of climate change where it disrupts established behaviours or introduces short-term costs. For example, efforts to introduce clean air zones in Greater Manchester sparked outrage and revolt from local residents unwilling to bear the costs of their polluting vehicles. The controversies surrounding attempts to establish clean air zones, or indeed any wider efforts to reduce traffic flows in different localities, are not easily surmountable. A refusal, at the individual level, to either alter behaviour or bear additional costs undermines any collective effort to tackle the problems that such behavioural change or financial levies aim to resolve. We could perhaps ask whether individuals should be responsible for the consequences of vehicles they bought in good faith or the actions they have been socialized into. Regardless, the consequences for those often least able to bear it will still be poorer health and shortened lifespans, with more deprived areas more likely to experience the highest levels of air pollution across the country.

The health and well-being of the population are not only directly implicated through the impact of climate change on weather and air quality but indirectly implicated through the sustainability of our health and social care system. In the autumn of 2020, NHS England became the world's first healthcare system to commit to reaching carbon net zero, cutting emissions across supply chains, facilities, clinical practice and more. To put this into perspective, consider that the level of carbon emissions for the NHS in England alone is equivalent to that of Denmark (Cameron *et al*. 2021). Central to the NHS's net zero ambitions are not only a wholesale change in how care is delivered but also substantial behaviour change among patients. For example, should the NHS prioritize disease prevention, this would reduce the need for carbon-intensive treatments (Cameron *et al*. 2021). An emphasis on disease prevention would follow from the sort of integrated system of health and social care outlined in Chapter 6. Climate has long been recognized as important for health; as far back as Hippocrates' work *On Airs, Waters and Places* in fact. But the pressures of our changing climate are not as yet central to thinking on how to provide welfare and why it is needed. Full commitment to the sustainability of the systems which support and provide welfare, as well as tackling the consequences of a changing and more hostile climate to our health and well-being, is imperative.

A DUD SILVER BULLET

The discovery of penicillin heralded unprecedented improvements to our life chances and longevity in illness and surgery. Where once even the tiniest of cuts to the finger could prove fatal if infection took hold, the growing availability of antibiotics since the discovery of penicillin all targeting bacterial infection revolutionized medicine, saving countless lives. But Sir Alexander Fleming, famed for his discovery of penicillin, foretold the crisis we now see in our fight against bacterial infection, warning in 1945 that the "public will demand [the drug and] ... then will begin an era of ... abuses" (cited in Ventola 2015). Overuse and misuse of medication, including simply forgetting to finish the full course of prescribed drugs, alongside stagnating efforts to develop new pharmaceutical interventions amid strict regulatory environments, have led to the emergence of resistant bacteria no longer curable with existing medications. One of the most well-known examples is MRSA, an infection that when on the skin is relatively treatable but if in the bloodstream is often fatal. Political attention to the crisis of emerging "superbugs" was, at least according to the scientific profession, woefully delayed. Although only relatively recently erupting into public and political debate, bacterial resistance to developing antibiotic treatments are as long established as the antibiotics themselves. George Orwell, for example, when writing *Nineteen Eighty-Four*, was apparently suffering from an antibiotic-resistant strain of tuberculosis. Nevertheless, it was the emergence of the superbugs that finally secured political interest. March 2013 saw then chief medical officer for the UK, Dame Sally Davies, publish a report into infections and the rise of antimicrobial resistance. She recommended that antibiotic resistance should be listed as a threat to national security alongside pandemic influenza and terrorism (Nature editorial 2013).

Humankind, it seems, is a victim of its own success. The medical advances that heralded the discovery and creation of highly effective antibiotics created the space in which we too often believe that a cure can be a prescribed pill. The silver bullet of medical intervention has led to the medicalization of society, in which we seek medical intervention in what, as Peter Conrad sets out, were once more typically viewed as normal human events (2007). Childbirth and ageing are particularly acute examples of this, but so too are the menopause, obesity and the insidious medicalization of well-being. Market forces rather than misplaced clinical attention drive this process as pharmaceutical industries exploit every opportunity to "fix" everyday suffering. The medicalization of society compromises the ability of health and social care systems to meet the demands of the populations they strive to support. But what is more problematic is that it creates dependency on healthcare systems to resolve some of the more ordinary pressures of everyday life that our social support networks, and a better-funded social care system, might otherwise have intervened in or even prevented. Consider the prevalence of multiple complex chronic health conditions in the population: Kate, a participant in Hilary Cottam's radical experiments to redesign different dimensions of the welfare state, is full-time carer to her husband and son, both with underlying health problems. And she herself has struggled as a consequence: she is "alone, overweight, diabetic, depressed and stuck" (Cottam 2018). In this situation, who do we turn to? Our confidence in the curative ability of our health care system wrought through the medicalization of our lives means we turn to our GPs. But that approach too often fails those with complex, chronic health conditions, particularly when mental health comes into play. Pharmaceuticals may not be the answer, but non-clinical services in the local community, coupled with strengthened informal social networks, may well be. In the face of antibacterial resistance, the adverse consequences of polypharmacy for older people and the limitations of clinical intervention in managing complex, chronic and multiple health conditions, an alternative to the now tarnished and broken silver bullet of medical intervention is needed.

WHAT NOW?

Throughout these pages, we have revisited the tensions between the prevailing neoliberal emphasis on the individual and the challenges this throws up in responsibility for and delivery of welfare. I am not the first to shine a light on these tensions. Hilary Cottam's works, for example – beginning with *Radical Help* and spanning the various manifestos she presents for a radically reimagined welfare system – consider this. In unpacking these tensions, Cottam turns to Aristotle's concept of *eudaimonia* or, as she describes it, human flourishing. Her arguments have helped shape the thoughts presented in these pages. Cottam urges a rediscovery of Aristotle's conception of human flourishing. The ability to flourish depends on collective participation in societal structures, beginning at home and extending through the marketplace across all of society's institutions. We are not individuals seeking to maximize individual gain, we are a collective working to foster human flourishing for all. What is wrong with our welfare system? It is "designed around who we imagine humans to be", as Cottam argues: "solitary, calculating and insatiable" maximizers of individual gain (2021: 11). We clearly recognize that we are not flourishing. But rather than fixing why, we simply buy into the economic systems that maintain this. The rising medicalization of normal human conditions is just one example of this. Alternatives do exist, and the rise in social prescribing as a route for general practitioners to refer those in need into non-clinical services in the local community is one good example of this. Sitting under the umbrella of community-centred approaches, these sorts of interventions have led to improvements in quality of life and in the emotional and mental well-being of participants. Challenges, however, remain. Where referral into what is typically provided by the voluntary and community sector in different localities severs responsibility for the consequences of unequal power structures for unequal life chances, we should resist. Community-based interventions must be properly and meaningfully funded, and developed in a wider context of recognition and action on unequal power and the social determinants of health. Only then can these sorts of interventions have a lasting effect on the inequalities and injustices of health and well-being today. If we are to rise to any new challenges wrought through the contemporary behemoth of disease, and to avert new crises, it is clearly time not only to re-imagine what humans should be but to fundamentally redesign the systems that support them.

8

Shoring up "Assumption B"

November 2022 marks 80 years since Beveridge's landmark report appeared. His proposals capitalized on the spirit of a population ravaged by war that was ready to work together to secure improved labour standards, economic advancement and social security for all. He was explicit in the importance of universality, refusing to be drawn by "sectional interests" and advocating for what truly was revolutionary. Rebuilding the country after the war was going to require an interlocking attack on all five giants. The report's "Assumption B" – that there would be a comprehensive national health service for all – underpinned the whole endeavour. But what of Assumption B today?

In 1942, the leading cause of death was "Other Myocardial Degeneration" (as defined by the International Classification of Disease). In other words, heart disease. It accounted for 8.1 per cent of all male deaths and 10.6 per cent of all female deaths. Cardiovascular health more broadly – other diseases of the heart and of blood vessels – accounted for an additional 8.8 per cent and 7.3 per cent of deaths for males and females, respectively. Among the remaining top ten leading causes of death were respiratory diseases such as bronchopneumonia and tuberculosis, strokes and cancers of the stomach for men and breast for women. Heart disease, lung disease and cancer remain global killers. But the giant of Disease evolved and so must our attack on it. Table

8.1 unpacks in more detail just how different that attack might need to be, comparing leading causes of death by age group and gender in 1942 and 2020. The burden of mental health is acutely visible in the prominence of suicide as a leading cause of death for younger ages today, but that is just the tip of the iceberg. And, were we interrogating data from 2019, for example, the toll of dementias in particular, but also cancers and heart disease, would also be visible. But more striking, given that once assumed transition through the age of receding pandemics, is the cost of Covid-19 in accounting for 12.9 per cent of all male deaths and 10.3 per cent of all female deaths.

There can be no greater signal for the need for change than the impact of a global pandemic in which millions lost their lives. But a revolution is needed when so many of those deaths were because of the toxicity of the social structures which characterize contemporary British society. Covid-19 capitalized on a crisis that had been long in the making. The primacy of the economy, the market and neoliberal principles have facilitated the rolling back of the welfare state, justified by the limits of public coffers and framed around the language of individual responsibility and fairness. In an address to the nation, Prime Minister Boris Johnson spoke of the many "needless" deaths to Covid-19. Needless is certainly right: so many of those deaths could and should have been prevented.

In June 2020, just a few months into the pandemic, it was estimated that as many as 17.8 per cent of individuals in the United States had medical debt (Kluender *et al.* 2021). The size of that debt increased between rich and poor areas, varying from just $126 to as much as $677. For many living in the UK, it is inconceivable to be saddled with medical debt. At the heart of Beveridge's proposals was a blueprint for a healthcare system that has been the pride and joy of many a Briton since its inception. The idea that a visit to the GP, the chemist or the hospital might cost more than the costs of a prescription are, because of his vision,

MALE				
Age	1942	% of male deaths	2020	% of female deaths
All ages	Heart disease (myo-cardial degeneration)	8.1	Covid-19	12.9
1–4	Respiratory disease (broncho-pneumonia)	12.7	Heart disease (con-genital heart disease)	3.8
5–19	Motor vehicle accident	10.1	Suicide	9.6
20–34	Respiratory disease (tuberculosis)	31.4	Suicide	16.7
50–64	Respiratory disease (tuberculosis)	17.3	Suicide	7.0
65–79	Heart disease (coronary arteries)	7.0	Covid-19	10.3
80+	Heart disease (myo-cardial degeneration)	11.3	Covid-19	12.9

FEMALE				
Age	1942	% of male deaths	2020	% of female deaths
All ages	Heart disease (myo-cardial degeneration)	10.6	Covid-19	10.3
1–4	Respiratory disease (broncho-pneumonia)	14.7	Sudden unexplained infant death syndrome	3.6
5–19	Respiratory disease (tuberculosis)	19.2	Suicide	8.9
20–34	Respiratory disease (tuberculosis)	33.0	Suicide	9.5
50–64	Respiratory disease (tuberculosis)	10.2	Breast cancer	12.5
65–79	Brain haemorrhage	9.9	Breast cancer	9.2
80+	Heart disease (myo-cardial degeneration)	13.0	Covid-19	10.1

Table 8.1   Leading causes of death by sex and age group, England and Wales, 1942 and 2020

Source: Office for National Statistics (2013, 2020b).

anathema. The NHS has since been envied the world over. If you fall and break your leg you do not debate the costs of getting it X-rayed and set, you go to A&E. If you are in pain or unwell, your biggest debate is whether to call the GP, see a pharmacist, consult 111 or go to hospital. The choices afforded to us because of Beveridge are truly remarkable, and it is that which the public cleaves to in its celebration of the realization of his Assumption B.

But the flagship of the welfare state, as we have seen, faltered as the costs and challenges of servicing a growing, more diverse, more aged and more expectant population rose. Every government since Beveridge's report has simply shored up the health and welfare system he outlined. The cost of the welfare state has been a political hot potato: just how much welfare provision is actually enough? These debates, and the resulting dismantling of Beveridge's welfare state, took on new urgency in the decade of fiscal austerity. During that period, the transfer of responsibility for social welfare from the state to the individual was disguised in the supposedly empowering language of the Big Society. Local communities and organizations were, according to this narrative, expected to grow their autonomy and ability to tackle the issues they faced head-on. It is right to emphasize the importance of local knowledge and understanding in tackling local issues. The remarkable and rapid emergence of local mutual aid groups in the wake of Covid-19 is just one example of the value and importance of that local knowledge and understanding. But even where local communities and groups are empowered to enact change, if the issues they tackle are created and exacerbated by uneven societal structures maintained by the state, responsibility for addressing them should be at the level of the state: politically and financially.

As successive governments have sought to navigate the economic, political and public minefield of NHS reform, their cuts and tinkering have stymied any real efforts to seek meaningful and radical change. Debate on welfare reform has, to date, sought to tread a fine line between discouraging free riders on the one hand

and indifference to poverty on the other. The result is piecemeal reform and the shoring up of a system designed for a population that no longer exists, slaying giants that have morphed in shape. To see healthcare as a right is no bad thing. If we fall ill, we should expect care, treatment and, where possible, cure. But too many of us erroneously assume that healthcare is the silver bullet for all of what ails us. Dismantling the structures through which violence is wrought is critical, but there are also practical, more immediate tasks ahead. However, there is a risk that the impact of Covid-19 and the universality to the experience – if not the consequences – of this pandemic will be used as a means to dismiss what surely is a new revolutionary moment in the world's history. Covid-19 was able to wreak the devastation it did because of the structures of our society and the shadow of austerity. Revolution is called for. Covid-19, and diseases like it, are able to emerge because of humankind's encroachment on the ever more fragile and ever more consumed global ecosystem. Revolution is called for. Any proposals for the future must consider the full experience of the past. To be a society free from want is also to be a society with a sustained attack on ignorance, idleness, squalor and disease. And, to achieve social security, this depends on cooperation between the state and the individual. So what are the conclusions of this survey of disease?

ASSUMPTION B.2

As vaccination programmes rolled out across countries of the Global North – to varying degrees of effect and uptake – many sanguinely looked to a "post-Covid" world in which business-as-usual would resume. Backs were turned to the plight of people and countries unable to meet the costs of mass vaccination, and the mildness of emerging strains of the virus were happily proclaimed. But business-as-usual should no longer be viable. For too long, global superpowers – including the UK – have given primacy to the individual and their role in maximizing GDP at the expense of attention to the more complex needs and more varied value of people, places and our planet. Not only does this give space for new disease vectors to emerge, it creates the noxious social conditions in which some struggle and perish while others thrive and prosper. We are, however, more than our economic output, and the world is more than a container for our economic activity.

Beveridge's vision has carried us as far as it can. The revolution it prompted is no longer sustainable in the face of demographic change. Foreshadowing the consolidation of capitalist, neoliberal values, the health and well-being of the population were a means to an end rather than an end in itself. A healthy, flourishing people were an economically prosperous nation but no longer. The complexity of our health and social care needs have increased, but reforms to health and social care have weakened the ability of those systems to meet the increasingly complex needs. The system as currently structured has already failed too many. Where once we pinned our hopes for health improvements – and therefore prosperity – on access to medical care, now we must collaborate on developments in social thinking. To prioritize economic growth and those who contribute to it is to simultaneously erode the health and well-being of society at large. We are simply creating more problems. It becomes a vicious, self-perpetuating and expanding cycle.

Galtung assumed that once structural violence – in which unequal life chances are determined by unequal power embedded in society – had been identified, the desire to tackle that violence would be "fairly consensual". The continued resonance of Galtung's thesis of 1969 belies such a consensus, but perhaps now, in the shadow of the pandemic, such a consensus is emerging? Political rhetoric touted by the government to "Build Back Better" and "Level Up" suggest recognition of the unfair chances in society for many people. But to me, it implies either a return to a previously approved state or at least a better version of it. That is not enough. We need to inspire consensus for a new status quo: one in which the individual matters more than their economic productivity, and one in which prosperity is more than economic well-being.

Galtung highlighted the tendency of societies to perpetuate patterns of inequality because of the hierarchical nature of their structure, and what that means for social, economic and political interactions within them. This will, he said, continue "unless deliberately and persistently prevented from doing so" (Galtung 1969: 77). You have read, in these pages, of a resounding lack of deliberate or persistent prevention. The Black Report of 1980 set out the limits of a national, comprehensive and free at the point of use health service. It could not prevent unequal life chances between the unskilled manual workers or their wives, and the professional men or indeed their wives. Attention to the material circumstances of these different classes and all in between was, according to the authors of the Black Report, urgently needed. Thatcher's administration buried that report and ignored its recommendations. Recommendations from the Marmot Review 30 years later were similarly urgent and similarly damning of the consequences of uneven social structures. But another ten years passed, and Sir Michael Marmot's revised, updated report saw nothing but a lost decade. His landmark review had been more than ignored. Cameron's austerity drive actively amplified the uneven social structures that Marmot's recommendations sought to rectify. We cannot rely on the hope of a five-year political mandate at each new general election. We need a consensus that is framed in more than the language of inequality.

Inequality can be, and has been, ignored by any whose wealth, income or self-esteem appears to buffer against it. But to have that bit more than your neighbour in a society of inequality is just to do that bit better than your neighbour. It is not to flourish. Remember, we are not living as long as our peers in many other high-income countries of the world. We are complicit in maintaining the violent structures of society that manifest in such unequal life chances because we do not demand that the political and economic elite dismantle them. If our tendency towards social stratification and inequality is a product of persistently repressive social structures, can a welfare state that should be premised on solidarity and collective action ever be possible? What is the alternative? What is more than patchy reform? First, a public consensus for action on our continued culpability for the early deaths of our children, the troubled existence of our adolescents and the pained, confused and struggling endurance of our grandparents. Second, an integrated system of welfare built out from the individual and the social networks that sustain them. Third, a new cooperation between the state and the individual that is not based on the primacy of economic growth and individual contribution to it.

Ultimately, "everything that we do to maintain, continue, and repair our 'world' so that we can live in it as well as possible" – to repeat Berenice Fisher and Joan Tronto's (1990: 40) famed definition of care – must now be central. Championed by the likes of the Women's Budget Group, among others, a care or caring economy would rise to the contemporary challenges of today while readying us for the emerging crises of tomorrow. Although resonant with Beveridge's emphasis on the social services needed to provide for the welfare of the people, it goes further. Care economies focus investment in public services: specifically those providing care for children, young people and older people. Chapters 4 and 5 laid bare the suffering and dismissal of many who should be in our care at either end of the life course. Inadequate, inappropriate care simply amplifies and perpetuates disadvantage over the life course, reproducing and magnifying inequalities within and between generations.

Sustained, targeted and substantial investment at all levels of the health *and* social care system would go far in improving not only the health of the population but also overall levels of well-being and life satisfaction. This has real economic benefit, but here health and well-being are both the means and the goal and are worth more than their instrumental value. We are capable of so much more, in all domains of life, when we have our health and the ability to manage and cope with ill-health, when we have our well-being and when we are content. If we are, like Beveridge, to underpin a new recovery and a new flourishing with an Assumption B, let Assumption B.2 drive forward from a national health *and* social care service adequately resourced to tackle more than the immediate costs of morbidity. Such a system of care means acknowledging that the suffering and dismissal of many at each end of the life course are not the only casualties of an economy in which all forms of care work, informal and formal, are secondary to wider macroeconomic planning and policy.

Economic growth is not only possible, but in fact equitable, in an economic system which prioritizes all forms of care sustaining life and the planet. Where high-quality care is planned and provided for within the economic system, the burden of unpaid care reduces and gendered inequalities – and their intersectional axes of inequality – narrow. Such an economy not only invests in all forms of care work, generating new jobs while bettering working conditions for all, it also attends to the social as well as the physical infrastructure. It would empower people and communities to meet challenges head-on with the full weight of social capital, resources and infrastructure which are better able to address so much of what ails us compared to the assumed silver bullet of medical, surgical or pharmacological intervention. It would, as the Women's Budget Group (2020) compellingly set out, achieve gender equality, sustainability and well-being. It categorically dismantles the violent structures of society and creates the space for collaborative, relational approaches to welfare provision while addressing uneven exposure to the social determinants of (ill-)health and (low) well-being. In these final pages, let us lay the foundations for the immediate tasks needed – looking in particular at just how much the population has changed – and the parameters for the transformation in social and political thinking and action needed. The book concludes with some concrete examples of where direct intervention is urgently needed and clearly absent: the final push for what is a call for more than patchy reform.

SINGLE, CHILDLESS AND AGEING

In 1942, Beveridge was among many in the political elites of society concerned with low levels of fertility in the population. People were simply not having enough children. On average, in Western societies such as the UK it is assumed that women need to have around 2.1 children over their childbearing lifespan to ensure that the population replenishes itself as older people die. This is known as "replacement-level fertility". But during the interwar years, fertility rates were well below replacement level, falling to as low as 1.72 in 1933 (Hobcraft 1996). A combination of the economic crises of the interwar years coupled with the stirrings of the sorts of ideational change in society that marked out the 1960s onwards are some of the factors behind these low levels of fertility. Unbeknown to Beveridge and his peers, however, fertility had begun to rise by the time he published his report. Nevertheless, his emphasis on raising a nation with the role of women set as mothers and carers, and men as workers and providers, characterizes the more paternalistic notions of gender and sex still prevalent today. Yet, despite wartime rises to fertility – notably among women aged 30 and over who had delayed childbirth during the Great Depression – and the subsequent birth of the generation now known as the baby boomers, fertility began to fall again. The ideational shifts that saw women stay on in education, enter the workforce and choose a path other than motherhood alone are, according to what is known as the second demographic transition, key factors driving these reductions to fertility (Lesthaeghe 2014). Not only did women feel freer to carve out a life defined by more than their ability to raise a child, but how people partnered and parented also changed. We marry less and later, and more often divorce, with concurrent rises to the numbers of people remaining single or cohabiting rather than legally partnering. There are more single people in older ages and more people choosing not to have or to have fewer children. The people and their needs, in 1942, were clearly very different from the people and their needs 80 years later.

As fertility rates have fallen, the concurrent increases to life expectancy have left the UK with a growing (for now) yet ageing population. The proportion of people aged 65 and over is increasing while the proportion of babies being born is not. This is a particular challenge to our system of welfare provision, which both pushes the bulk of the responsibility for care of dependent groups into the private realms of people's family and personal lives while also disinvesting in and rolling back the public support networks that can bolster that home-based care. If fewer babies are being born, and the workforce itself is ageing, who is moving into that workforce to fill positions in the labour market? Artificial intelligence and the automatization of many a role may close some gaps, but there are roles in education, social care and health care, to name but a few sectors, that cannot be accomplished by machine or computer. Will there be enough people paying into the tax system upon which much of our provision of welfare is based, if the workforce is shrinking while health and social care needs also become more complex and more expensive?

Many will already have faced the challenges of caring for an aged parent or grandparent, no doubt complicated by the fact that many of us also move away from where we grew up and where our parents live. And what of those whose parents divorced, remarried or repartnered? If you are a single child but have as many as two sets of parents to care for, how do you divide your time? The scandal of older adult social care so regularly featured in our newspapers means that many may be reluctant to turn to stretched local authority service provision. What does exist may not be enough, even if that is your only option. What remains then falls to the individual. Although the challenges of care provision are no less acute now than in Beveridge's day, the need for a care-led recovery and care-based economy has never been greater. As the balance of young to old shifts, the nature of care needs and requirements of care provision alters. The full gamut of care services – including residential and day-based child and older person care, healthcare, personal social and domestic services, and education – needs to be resourced within the context of local need. Nationally, no one group should take precedence in a society which must promote intergenerational harmony. Yet locally, provision must be sensitive to the structure of local and changing populations, building on the wealth of community knowledge and understanding too often dismissed from decision-making, policy development and service planning.

KEEPING PACE

Health and social care systems have not kept pace with changes in the composition of our population: we are older and we are more ethnically diverse than ever before. But there is also an internal conflict between our health and social care systems. This can, for example, be seen in the tensions between the successes of antibacterial drug development and the dependency that has been manufactured in contemporary society as to the need for a "pill" to fix and cure all. As we lean on the healthcare system, we forget and neglect the systems of social care, formalized and personal, that may better intervene in or prevent much of what ails us. A trickier conflict, however, has emerged because of the incredible advances in medical technology that means some who may once not have survived the first days, months or years of their life now live far into adulthood. To be born today with a profound and multiple learning disability offers a chance of life that, pre-Beveridge and the advances of health and medical care, were unimaginable.

This is to be celebrated, but our provision of social care to support these children as they grow up and age has not kept pace with the health care that ensures their chances of life. Provision for special educational needs schooling is patchy and inadequate, but the invaluable support that is offered to the children and their parents or carers largely ceases once that child reaches 18. The care required is then down to the capacity and resources of their parents and family, with little to no support from the state. A pressing and looming problem is what happens to these children, who can flourish with support and appropriate care, once their carer – typically a parent – dies?

Beveridge remarked that the coming of old age is inevitable and can be and is to a large extent foreseen. Yet the system he designed is clearly not capable of supporting our current aged population, let alone one that will continue to age. Successive governments have kicked the can down the road when they could have done more, positioning young alongside old in debates of welfare provision and support rather than setting them up in opposition to each other. The short-sighted marginalization of older people, particularly those who will inevitably cost more because they have, to date, already been marginalized, must not be repeated as we look to the changing composition of the population of today.

DEPOLITICIZING THE INDIVIDUAL

The demographic changes of the 1960s onwards are in line with the growing political emphasis on the individual. In sociological literature, this is made explicit in discussions of the individualization of the life course (e.g. Beck & Beck-Gernsheim 2002). Rather than strict adherence to societal norms and traditions, we can live our lives to please ourselves. Where this gives people the freedom to flourish, it is a boon. And yet, constrained by the societal parameters of neoliberalism and capitalism, that freedom to flourish is often uneven and only really possible if directed in a specific way. Women have gained a lot since 1942, for example, but are they really so free to live their lives as they please? The expansion to the care burden they disproportionately shouldered during the Covid-19 pandemic suggests not. But women are not the only ones who see their capacity to live their lives just as they please curtailed in contemporary society. Consider what it means to live with a disability, or to be Black, Brown or in some way minoritized by the structures of society. Consider too just how free you are to live as you like if your income is low or if the context of your lives, your work or your opportunities for recreation are ones of deprivation. The people who are able to live just as they like are the ones who are seen to hold most value in our emphatically neo-liberal, capitalist society.

It is they who reap the rewards of investment in infrastructure, in service provision and in schooling. Their return on that public investment is high: high incomes, secure homes, secure jobs and the associated good health and longevity. That their return on this public investment would actually be greater if they lived in a less unequal society seems to have largely escaped them. Why else would they remain complicit in maintaining the structures that advantage them at the expense of others? Political emphasis on the individual makes the individual a driver of economic prosperity. Invest in their ability to contribute to the economy, and by earning more money they contribute more to it. But this framing of the economic value of an individual not only devalues those who, for whatever reason, are less able to contribute, it also devalues the work of anyone without a tangible economic value. I use the word "tangible" advisably. There is far more "work" of value than there is work which has a tangible economic outcome. Care is a prime example.

The trend towards individualization has eroded our sense of shared ownership and vested interest in our ailing system of welfare support. We are persuaded that responsibility for poor health and low well-being, beyond things like the broken hip or failing heart, rests with the individual. Why then should the hard-working taxpayer cover the spiralling costs of complex, chronic conditions? We are persuaded that the system is ailing because too many of us are expecting more than we deserve, which is evidenced by the fact that when told not to use the NHS during the pandemic, many people did to lethal effect. The language of Beveridge's five giants – squalor, disease, idleness, want and ignorance – conjures a certain picture of those needing state help. It does not conjure the idea of a person, family or community constrained by the structures of society, the working single-mother, the pensioner who lost their savings in a pension fraud or the learning-disabled adult. The image is of the filthy home of an ignorant, lazy, work-shy benefit scrounger. We assume that all can be an able, self-maximizing, economic actors. But we should resist the political misappropriation of the idea and value of the individual, along with the political misappropriation of the concept of fairness. Neither should be used to justify shrinking welfare provision or to demonize those already marginalized.

MORE THAN PATCHY REFORM

Inequality – the product of a structurally violent system – drives health problems in our society. Uneven access to power, resources and opportunities have transformed the nature of what ails us, which is made all too visible in the changes to what kills us. For Beveridge, what was missing in efforts to provide for the health and well-being of the population was not only access to suitable healthcare but some form of national coordination to this provision embedded within a multipronged attack on all five giants barring the road to reconstruction and recovery. Although necessary, this is no longer sufficient. Just as the giant of Disease has evolved and morphed, so too has the composition and size of the population it stalks. A one-size-fits-all approach is neither appropriate nor adequate given the spatial hetero-geneity to society and the complexities of what inform and shape individual- and community-level health and well-being. A visit to the GP is not the solution for all that ails us. Yet gaps in our care system and misguided public expectations of the role of our GPs – even aside from the difficulties some face in visiting GPs – maintains this erroneous belief in the silver bullet offered by the NHS.

We often talk of a health and social care system, but still public assumptions and the flow of resources perpetuate the primacy of medical, surgical and pharmacological intervention in our care provision. We need to simultaneously separate preventative and curative care across physical and mental health, social care needs and well-being across the life course, while also maintaining conversation, dialogue and interaction within and between these nodes of care. A GP cannot solve everything, but they should have access to and knowledge of alternative care options, whether preventative or curative, in the local community. Accordingly, care at all levels must be provided in line with need. Although many of us are familiar with the often-repeated north–south divide, the geography of inequality in social, economic and health outcomes is far more mountainous. Our health and well-being is embedded within the communities in which we live, work, age, play and grow. Responses to it should also be so embedded, as the knowledge of our local directors of public health and the actions of our local mutual aid groups made only too clear during Covid-19. National coordination is important, but just as health and well-being vary regionally and locally so must the nature and coordination of care. Julian Tudor Hart's famous inverse care law is worthy of re-examination: Covid-19 exposed new fault lines to the geography of care and support which only a nationally resourced but locally coordinated, managed and delivered response can tackle.

It remains to be seen whether the emergence and experience of Covid-19 can be the pivot point for transformative societal change so many hope and urge for. But the learning opportunities offered by looking at our provision of care through the lens of Covid-19 cannot be ignored. National lockdowns and over-whelmed, reoriented care services – in health, social services and education – eroded some of the basic provisions or entitlements Beveridge's system once it had been created. Prime examples that will have a long reach into the lives of the babies and children of the Covid-19 years include ready access to home-based midwifery care or the support for childhood development, including the identification of early signals of learning difficulties and speech impediments. But this is a chronic problem simply made acute. We saw in Chapter 6 the consequences of disinvestment and underfunding in healthcare and training through impacts on mid-wifery and nursing. Healthcare visitors have also seen dramatic reductions: falling, for example, by 35 per cent between December 2015 and December 2020. Across the board, high workloads and shrinking workforces undermine the ability of healthcare work-ers to provide meaningful, engaged care. For those working in the community, the combined effect of increasing workloads and shrinking workforces is particularly toxic, compromising the abil-ity to build relationships, networks and trust. The preventative strand of our health and social care system has been progressively weakened and eroded since Beveridge first created the space to build it. In the context of an aged and ageing population, where the health of our children and young people is characterized by obesity and mental illness, this erosion of community support is ever more noxious. Where the fatness of our children leads to poorer health outcomes and lower well-being, for example, sim-ply imposing a "sugar tax" or condemning "poor parenting" will not be sufficient to address this. Rather, it depends on meaning-ful community-based support embedded within a wider effort to dismantle the violent structures perpetuating constrained food and nutrition choices. The presence of such community support networks must then extend across the life course, supporting and enabling positive health outcomes for young and old.

The national coordination of targeted funding within a model that prioritizes local knowledge, community networks and understanding are essential to the meaningful provision of care to all in need, and of pre-emptive support for all in life. To provide for the welfare of contemporary society is to care for all people in it and for the planet that houses it. Our Assumption B.2 is one premised on a care economy in which care is community-led, valued and reciprocal. It is premised on a society committed to dismantling the violent structures through which unequal life chances and opportunities are maintained and perpetuated: one that would follow from a care-based economy. Covid-19 has shown the continued value of Beveridge's vision and of his emphasis on a combined attack on his five giants. But it has also highlighted the need for a true and fundamental reforming of that vision. Responsibility for the consequences of a structurally violent society, and for redistributing the unequal power that leads to unequal life chances, should rest with the political and economic elite whose interests are protected and maintained by those violent structures. But we are culpable too. Our attack on Beveridge's giants will not be couched in language that frames their consequences as the shortcomings of the individual. We must, as Beveridge did, learn from the full experiences of the past. We can unite in an attack on the five giants whose presence still blocks the path for too many today. And we can rethink what it means to achieve cooperation between the state and the individual. Revolution is needed now.

References

Abbasi, A, *et al.* (2017). "Body mass index and incident type 1 and type 2 diabetes in children and young adults: a retrospective cohort study". *Journal of the Endocrine Society* 1(5): 524–37.

Age UK (2019). "Briefing: health and care of older people in England 2019". https://www.ageuk.org.uk/globalassets/age-uk/documents/reports-and-publications/reports-and-briefings/health--wellbeing/age_uk_briefing_state_of_health_and_care_of_older_people_july2019.pdf.

Appleby, J. & R. Thorlby (2008). "Data briefing: waiting times are just so … 1950s". The Kings Fund. https://www.kingsfund.org.uk/publications/articles/data-briefing-waiting-times-are-just-so1950s.

Bambra, C. (2016). *Health Divides: Where You Live Can Kill You*. Bristol: Policy Press.

Bambra, C. *et al.* (2020). "The Covid-19 pandemic and health inequalities". *Journal of Epidemiology and Community Health* 74(11): 964–8.

Barnett, K. *et al.* (2012). "Epidemiology of multimorbidity and implications for health care, research, and medical education: a cross-sectional study". *The Lancet* 380: 37–43.

Baylis, M. (2017). "Potential impact of climate change on emerging vector-borne and other infections in the UK". *Environmental Health* 16 (Suppl. 1): 112.

BBC News (2021). "Chard flooding: people rescued and homes damaged". https://www.bbc.co.uk/news/uk-england-somerset-57649276.

Bean, W. (1957). "Fibrocystic disease of the pancreas". *AMA Arch Internal Medicine* 99(2): 321–2.

Beck, U. & E. Beck-Gernsheim (2002). *Individualization: Institutionalized Individualism and Its Social and Political Consequences*. London: Sage.

Beveridge, W. (1942). *Social Insurance and Allied Services*. London: HM Stationary Office.

Blanchard, S. (2020). "SAGE warned the Government 'very early on' in Britain's coronavirus outbreak that care homes would be COVID-19 hotspots, chief scientific advisor reveals". *Mail Online*, 27 April. https://www.dailymail.co.uk/news/article-8261149/SAGE-warned-Government-early-care-homes-risk-COVID-19.html.

British Medical Association (BMA) (2020). "Social care in Northern Ireland". https://www.bma.org.uk/advice-and-support/nhs-delivery-and-workforce/social-care/social-care-in-northern-ireland.

Butler, P. (2020). "'He was fit for hospital, now for work': the people failed by the benefits system". *The Guardian*, 7 February. https://www.theguardian.com/society/2020/feb/07/three-cases-of-suicides-linked-to-dwps-handling-of-benefits.

Cadar, D. *et al.* (2018). "Individual and area-based socioeconomic factors associated with dementia incidence in England: evidence from a 12-year follow-up in the English longitudinal study of ageing". *JAMA Psychiatry* 75(7): 723–32.

Cameron, G., A. Göpfert & T. Gardner (2021). "Going green: what do the public think about the NHS and climate change?" The Health Foundation. https://www.health.org.uk/publications/long-reads/going-green-what-do-the-public-think-about-the-nhs-and-climate-change.

Campbell, D. (2018). "People must take responsibility for own health, says Matt Hancock". *The Guardian*, 5 November. https://www.theguardian.com/society/2018/nov/05/people-must-take-responsibility-for-own-health-says-matt-hancock. .

Care Quality Commission (2020). "Review of do not attempt cardiopulmonary resuscitation decisions during the COVID-19 pandemic". https://www.cqc.org.uk/sites/default/files/20201204%20DNACPR%20Interim%20Report%20-%20FINAL.pdf.

Carney, G. & P. Nash (2020). *Critical Questions for Ageing Societies*. Bristol: Policy Press.

Cassell, A. *et al.* (2018). "The epidemiology of multimorbidity in primary care: a retrospective cohort study". *British Journal of General Practice* 68(669): e245–51.

Centre for Ageing Better (2021). "Boom and bust? The last baby

boomers and their prospects for later life". https://ageing-better.org.
uk/sites/default/files/2021–11/boom-and-bust-report-the-last-
baby-boomers.pdf.

Chadwick, E. (1842). *Report on the Sanitary Condition of the Labouring
Population of Great Britain*. London.

Chambers Dictionary of Etymology (2008). Edinburgh: Chambers Harrap
Publishers Ltd.

Charlesworth, A. (2021). "Staff shortages left the NHS vulnerable to the
COVID-19 storm". The Health Foundation. https://www.health.org.
uk/news-and-comment/blogs/staff-shortages-left-the-nhs-
vulnerable-to-the-covid-19-storm.

Collishaw, S. *et al.* (2010). "Trends in adolescent emotional problems in
England: a comparison of two national cohorts twenty years apart".
Journal of Child Psychology and Psychiatry 51(8): 885–94.

Commission on Race and Ethnic Disparities (2021). *Commission on Race
and Ethnic Disparities: The Report*. https://assets.publishing.service.
gov.uk/government/uploads/system/uploads/attachment_data/
file/974507/20210331_-_CRED_Report_-_FINAL_-_Web_
Accessible.pdf.

Conrad, P. (2007). *The Medicalization of Society: On the Transformation
of Human Conditions into Treatable Disorders*. Baltimore, MD: Johns
Hopkins University Press.

Cottam, H. (2018). *Radical Help: How We Can Remake the Relationships
between Us and Revolutionise the Welfare State*. London: Virago.

Cottam, H. (2021). "A radical new vision for social care". The Health
Foundation. https://reader.health.org.uk/a-radical-new-vision-
for-social-care.

Department of Health (n.d.). "No health without mental health: a cross-
government mental health outcomes strategy for people of all ages".
https://assets.publishing.service.gov.uk/government/uploads/
system/uploads/attachment_data/file/215808/dh_123993.pdf.

Department of Health and Social Care (2021). "Integration and
innovation: working together to improve health and social
care for all". https://www.gov.uk/government/publications/
working-together-to-improve-health-and-social-care-for-all/
integration-and-innovation-working-together-to-improve-
health-and-social-care-for-all-html-version.

Department of Health and Social Security (1980). *Inequalities in Health:
Report of a Research Working Group*. London: DHSS.

Diernberger, K. *et al.* (2021). "Healthcare use and costs in the last year
of life: a national population data linkage study". *BMJ Support
Palliative Care* 12: 002708.

Donnelly, L. & G. Rayner (2020). "Lose 5lbs save NHS money, says Matt Hancock after UK's coronavirus wake-up call". *The Telegraph*, 26 July. https://www.telegraph.co.uk/politics/2020/07/26/lose-5lb-save-nhs-100m-says-matt-hancock-coronavirus-wake-up/.

Dorling, D. (2017). "Life expectancy in Britain has stagnated, meaning that a million years of life could disappear by 2058 – why?" *The Independent*, 28 December. https://www.independent.co.uk/voices/uk-life-expectancy-drops-2058-government-cuts-austerity-nhs-national-health-a8131526.html.

Dyer, C. (2022). "Covid-19: government's use of VIP lane for awarding PPE contracts was unlawful says judge". *BMJ* 276: o96.

Feinstein, A. (1970). "The pre-therapeutic classification of co-morbidity in chronic disease". *Journal of Chronic Disease* 23: 455–68.

Fisher, B. & J. Tronto (1990). "Towards a feminist theory of care". In E. Abel & M. Neslon (eds), *Circles of Care*. Albany, NY: SUNY Press.

Galtung, J. (1969). "Violence, peace, and peace research". *Journal of Peace Research* 6(3): 167–91.

Green, M., D. Dorling & J. Minton (2017a). "The geography of a rapid rise in elderly mortality in England and Wales, 2014–15". *Journal of Health and Place* 44: 77–85.

Green, M. *et al.* (2017b). "Could the rise in mortality rates since 2015 be explained by changes in the number of delayed discharges of NHS patients?" *Journal of Epidemiology and Community Health* 71: 1068–71.

Grover, C. (2019). "Violent proletarianisation: social murder, the reserve army of labour and social security 'austerity' in Britain". *Critical Social Policy* 39(3): 335–55.

Halliday, J. (2020). "Lockdown tightened in parts of northern England with ban on indoor meetings". *The Guardian*, 30 July. https://www.theguardian.com/uk-news/2020/jul/30/lockdown-tightened-in-parts-of-northern-england-with-ban-on-indoor-meetings.

Hamnett, C. (2013). "Shrinking the welfare state: the structure, geography and impact of British government benefit cuts". *Transactions of the Institute of British Geographers* 39(4): 490–503.

Harpur, A. *et al.* (2021). "Trends in infant mortality and still birth rates in Scotland by socio-economic position, 2000–2018: a longitudinal ecological study". *BMC Public Health* 21(995): 1–14.

Hart, J. (1971). "The inverse care law". *The Lancet* 297(7696): 405–12.

Hiam, L. *et al.* (2018). "Why is life expectancy in England and Wales 'stalling'?" *Journal of Epidemiology and Community Health* 72(5): 404–8.

Hill, A. (2021). "Young mental health referrals double in England after lockdowns". *The Guardian*, 15 July. https://www.theguardian.com/society/2021/jul/15/young-mental-health-referrals-double-in-england-after-lockdowns.

Hobcraft, J. (1996). "Fertility in England and Wales: a fifty-year perspective". *Population Studies* 50(3): 485–524.

Honigsbaum, M. (2020). *The Pandemic Century: A History of Global Contagion from the Spanish Flue to Covid-19*. London: Penguin.

IPSOS Mori (2019). "NHS leads as top election issue with Conservatives still expected to be largest party". https://www.ipsos.com/ipsos-mori/en-uk/nhs-leads-top-election-issue-conservatives-still-expected-be-largest-party.

Jardine, J. *et al.* (2021). "Adverse regency outcomes attributable to socioeconomic and ethnic inequalities in England: a national cohort study". *The Lancet* 398(10314): 1905–12.

Kluender, R., N. Mahoney & F. Wong (2021). "Medical debt in the US, 2009–2020". *JAMA* 326(3): 250–56.

Krelle, H. & C. Tallack (2021). "One year on: three myths about COVID-19 that the data proved wrong". The Health Foundation. https://www.health.org.uk/publications/long-reads/one-year-on-three-myths-about-COVID-19-that-the-data-proved-wrong.

Kröger, H., E. Pakpahan & R. Hoffman (2015). "What causes health inequality? A systematic review on the relative importance of social causation and health selection". *European Journal of Public Health* 25(6): 951–60.

Kuh, D. & Y. Ben-Shlomo (1997). *A Life Course Approach to Chronic Disease Epidemiology: Tracing the Origins of Ill-Health from Early to Adult Life*. Oxford: Oxford University Press.

Lesthaeghe, R. (2014). "The second demographic transition: a concise overview of its development". *PNAS* 111(51): 18112–15.

Levy, B. *et al.* (2002). "Longevity increased by positive self-perceptions of ageing". *Journal Personality and Social Psychology* 83(2): 261–70.

Levy, B. *et al.* (2020). "Ageism amplifies cost and prevalance of health conditions". *The Gerontologist* 60(1): 174–81.

Local Government Association (2019). "CAMHS: facts and figures". https://www.local.gov.uk/about/campaigns/bright-futures/bright-futures-camhs/child-and-adolescent-mental-health-and.

Loopstra, R. *et al.* (2016). "Austerity and old-age mortality in England: a longitudinal cross-local area analysis, 2007–2013". *Journal of the Royal Society of Medicine* 109(3): 108–16.

Luta, X. *et al.* (2020). "Healthcare trajectories and costs in the last year of life: a retrospective primary care and hospital analysis". *BMJ Support Palliative Care* 2: 002630.

Marmot, M. (2005). "Social determinants of health". *The Lancet* 365(9646): 1099–104.

Marmot, M. *et al.* (2020). "Health equity in England: the Marmot Review 10 years on". Institute of Health Equity and The Health Foundation. https://www.health.org.uk/publications/reports/the-marmot-review-10-years-on.

May, C. (1944). "Fibrosis of the pancreas in infants and children". *Proceeding of the Royal Society of Medicine* 37(7): 311–13.

Mwamba R (2021). "The Christmas I lost everything . . . and how it changed my life". *Manchester Evening News.* https://www.manchestereveningnews.co.uk/news/greater-manchester-news/the-christmas-lost-everything-how-22545884.

Nath, S., P. Hardelid & A. Zylbersztejn (2021). "Are infant mortality rates increasing in England? The effect of extreme prematurity and early neonatal deaths". *Journal of Public Health* 43(3): 541–50.

National Records of Scotland (2019). "Vital events reference tables – deaths". https://www.nrscotland.gov.uk/statistics-and-data/statistics/statistics-by-theme/vital-events/general-publications/vital-events-reference-tables/2019/list-of-data-tables.

National Records of Scotland (2019). "Mid-2019 population estimates Scotland". https://www.nrscotland.gov.uk/statistics-and-data/statistics/statistics-by-theme/population/population-estimates/mid-year-population-estimates/mid-2019.

Nature editorial (2013). "The antibiotic alarm". *Nature* 495(7440): 141.

NHS Digital (2021). "National child measurement programme, England 2020/21 school year". https://digital.nhs.uk/data-and-information/publications/statistical/national-child-measurement-programme/2020-21-school-year.

NIHR (2018). "Multi-morbidity predicted to increase in the UK over the next 20 years". https://evidence.nihr.ac.uk/alert/multi-morbidity-predicted-to-increase-in-the-uk-over-the-next-20-years/.

Obesity Action Scotland (2021). "Protecting Scotland's children: is taking childhood obesity more vital than ever?" https://www.obesityactionscotland.org/blog/protecting-scotland-s-children-is-tackling-childhood-obesity-more-vital-than-ever/.

Odd, D. *et al.* (2021). "Child mortality and social deprivation". National Child Mortality Database. https://www.ncmd.info/wp-content/uploads/2021/05/NCMD-Child-Mortality-and-Social-Deprivation-report_20210513.pdf.

OECD (n.d.). "Nursing graduates". https://data.oecd.org/healthres/nursing-graduates.htm.

Office for National Statistics (2015). "How has life expectancy

changed over time?" https://www.ons.gov.uk/
peoplepopulationandcommunity/birthsdeathsandmarriages/
lifeexpectancies/articles/howhaslifeexpectancychangedovertime/
2015-09-09.

Office for National Statistics (2018). "Excess winter mortality in
England and Wales 2017 to 2018 (provisional) and 2016 to 2017
(final)". https://www.ons.gov.uk/peoplepopulationandcommunity/
birthsdeathsandmarriages/deaths/bulletins/
excesswintermortalityinenglandandwales/2017to2018
provisionaland2016to2017final.

Office for National Statistics (2019). "Live births and infant
deaths by NS-SEC (2011–2017), and IMD (2008 to 2017)".
https://www.ons.gov.uk/peoplepopulationandcommunity/
birthsdeathsandmarriages/deaths/adhocs/010121livebirthsand
infantdeathsbynssec2011to2017andimd2008to2017.

Office for National Statistics (2020a). "National life tables England and
Wales". https://www.ons.gov.uk/peoplepopulationandcommunity/
birthsdeathsandmarriages/lifeexpectancies/datasets/
nationallifetablesenglandandwalesreferencetables.

Office for National Statistics (2020b). "Leading causes
of death, UK: 2001–2018". https://www.ons.gov.uk/
peoplepopulationandcommunity/healthandsocialcare/
causesofdeath/articles/leadingcausesofdeathuk/2001to2018.

Office for National Statistics (2020c). "Child poverty and
education outcomes by ethnicity". https://www.ons.
gov.uk/economy/nationalaccounts/uksectoraccounts/
compendium/economicreview/february2020/
childpovertyandeducationoutcomesbyethnicity.

Office for National Statistics (2021a). "National Life Tables".
https://www.ons.gov.uk/peoplepopulationandcommunity/
healthandsocialcare/causesofdeath/articles/
leadingcausesofdeathuk/2001to2018.

Office for National Statistics (2021b). "Vital statistics in the UK: births,
deaths and marriages". https://www.ons.gov.uk/
peoplepopulationandcommunity/populationandmigration/
populationestimates/datasets/
vitalstatisticspopulationandhealthreferencetables.

Office for National Statistics (2021c). "Life expectancy for local
areas of the UK: between 2000 to 2003 and 2018 to 2020".
https://www.ons.gov.uk/peoplepopulationandcommunity/
healthandsocialcare/healthandlifeexpectancies/datasets/
lifeexpectancyestimatesallagesuk.

Oldfield, P. (2021). "'The future used to be exciting . . . now it's frightening': life on the Salford streets where families live one bill away from disaster". *Manchester Evening News*, 1 November. https://www.manchestereveningnews.co.uk/news/greater-manchester-news/the-future-used-exciting-now-22008362.

Oliver, I. (2021). "Understanding the health effects of climate change". UK Health Security Agency. https://ukhsa.blog.gov.uk/2021/11/09/understanding-the-health-effects-of-climate-change/.

Olshanksy, S. & A. Ault (1986). "The fourth stage of the epidemiologic transition: the age of delayed degenerative diseases". *Milbank Quarterly* 64(3): 355–91.

Omran, A. (1971). "The epidemiological transition: a theory of the epidemiology of population change". *Milbank Quarterly* 49(4): 509–38.

OpenSafely (2021). "Vaccination rates by age and area deprivation". https://github.com/opensafely/nhs-covid-vaccination-coverage/tree/main/released-outputs/machine_readable_outputs/table_csvs.

Opondo, C. *et al.* (2019). "Joint contribution of socioeconomic circumstances and ethnic group to variations in preterm birth, neonatal mortality and infant mortality in England and Wales: a population-based retrospective cohort study using routine data from 2006 to 2012". *BMJ Open* 9(7): e028227.

Palmer, B. (2019). "Is the number of GPs falling across the UK?" Nuffield Trust. https://www.nuffieldtrust.org.uk/news-item/is-the-number-of-gps-falling-across-the-uk#checking-the-vital-signs-for-general-practice.

Perry, R. *et al.* (2021). "Exploring high mortality rates among people with multiple and complex needs: a qualitative study using peer research methods". *BMJ Open* 11: e044634.

Press, C. (2020). "Coronavirus: the NHS workers wearing bin bags as protection". *BBC News*, 5 April. https://www.bbc.co.uk/news/health-52145140.

Public Health England (2021). "Health Profile for England". https://fingertips.phe.org.uk/static-reports/health-profile-for-england/hpfe_report.html#summary-5---life-expectancy.

Public Health England (n.d.). "Local authority health profiles". https://fingertips.phe.org.uk/profile/health-profiles/data#page/7/gid/8000073/pat/6/par/E12000001/ati/201/are/E06000047/iid/92196/age/2/sex/4/cat/-1/ctp/-1/yrr/3/cid/4/tbm/1/page-options/ine-yo-3:2018:-1:-1_ine-pt-0_ine-ct-115.

Public Health Scotland (2020). "Primary 1 Body Mass Index

(BMI) statistics Scotland. School year 2019 to 2020". https://
  publichealthscotland.scot/publications/primary-1-body-
  mass-index-bmi-statistics-scotland/primary-1-body-mass-
  index-bmi-statistics-scotland-school-year-2019-to-2020/.
Public Health Wales NHS Trust (2019). "Every child measurement
  programme 2017/18". http://www.wales.nhs.uk/sitesplus/
  documents/888/CMP%20report%20%28Eng%29.pdf.
Pybus, K. *et al*. (2021). "'How do I make something out of nothing?':
  universal credit, precarity and mental health". Covid
  Realities. https://covidrealities.org/learnings/write-ups/
  universal-credit-precarity-and-mental-health.
Raleigh, V. (2018). "Stalling life expectancy in the UK". *BMJ*
  362(4050). https://www.kingsfund.org.uk/publications/
  stalling-life-expectancy-uk.
Rawlinson, K. (2020). "Coronavirus PPE: all 40,000 gowns flown from
  Turkey for NHS fail UK standards". *The Guardian*, 7 May. https://
  www.theguardian.com/world/2020/may/07/all-400000-
  gowns-flown-from-turkey-for-nhs-fail-uk-standards.
Robertson-Molloy, J. (2021). "Threadbare social services have lost
  the trust of families". *The Guardian*, Letters, 4 June. https://www.
  theguardian.com/society/2021/jun/04/threadbare-social-
  services-have-lost-the-trust-of-families.
Royal College of Midwives (2016). "Budget cuts, service cuts, staffing
  shortages = maternity services in 2016". https://www.rcm.org.uk/
  media-releases/2016/october/budget-cuts-service-cuts-staffing-
  shortages-maternity-services-in-2016/.
Royal College of Midwives (2021). "RCM warns of midwife exodus as
  maternity staffing crisis grows". https://www.rcm.org.uk/media-
  releases/2021/september/rcm-warns-of-midwife-exodus-as-
  maternity-staffing-crisis-grows/.
Royal College of Paediatrics and Child Health (2020). "State of child
  health in the UK". https://stateofchildhealth.rcpch.ac.uk.
Royal College of Physicians (2016). "Every breath we take: the lifelong
  impact of air pollution". https://www.rcplondon.ac.uk/projects/
  outputs/every-breath-we-take-lifelong-impact-air-pollution.
Ryan, F. (2019). *Crippled: Austerity and the Demonization of Disabled
  People*. London: Verso.
Sanchez-Graells, A. (2020a). "The PPE scandal shines a light on the
  worrying future of UK procurement law". LSE British Politics
  and Policy Blog. https://blogs.lse.ac.uk/politicsandpolicy/
  ppe-scandal-procurement-law/.
Sanchez-Graells, A. (2020b). "COVID-19 PPE extremely urgent

procurement in England: a cautionary tale for an overheating public governance". https://papers.ssrn.com/sol3/papers.cfm?abstract_id=3711526.

Scobie, S. (2021). "Covid-19 and the deaths of care home residents". Nuffield Trust. https://www.nuffieldtrust.org.uk/news-item/covid-19-and-the-deaths-of-care-home-residents.

Shilliam, R. (2018). *Race and the Undeserving Poor: From Abolition to Brexit*. Newcastle upon Tyne: Agenda.

Singer, L. *et al.* (2019). "Social determinants of multimorbidity and multiple functional limitations among the ageing population of England, 2002–2015". *SSM Population Health* 8: 100413.

Singer, M. (1996). "A dose of drugs, a touch of violence, a case of AIDS: conceptualizing the Sava Syndemic". *Free Inquiry – Special Issue: Gangs, Drugs & Violence* 24(2): 99–110.

Sinha, I. *et al.* (2021). "Ignoring systemic racism hinders efforts to eliminate health inequalities in childhood". *BMJ Opinion*. https://blogs.bmj.com/bmj/2021/04/27/ignoring-systemic-racism-hinders-efforts-to-eliminate-racial-health-inequalities-in-childhood/.

Social Metrics Commission (2018). "A new measure of poverty for the UK". https://socialmetricscommission.org.uk/wp-content/uploads/2019/07/SMC_measuring-poverty-201809_full-report.pdf.

Standing, G. (2011). *The Precariat: The Dangerous New Class*. London: Bloomsbury.

Statista (2021). "Number of confirmed malaria cases in Africa as of 2020, by country". https://www.statista.com/statistics/1239998/number-of-confirmed-malaria-cases-in-africa-by-country/.

Szreter, S. (1997). "Economic growth, disruption, deprivation, disease, and death: on the importance of the politics of public health for development". *Population and Development Review* 23(4): 693–728.

Taylor-Robinson, D. *et al.* (2019). "Assessing the impact of rising child poverty on the unprecedented rise in infant mortality in England, 2000–2017: time trend analysis". *BMJ Open* 9: e028424.

The Lancet (2017). "Syndemics: health in context". *The Lancet* 389(10072): 881.

Timmins, N. (2017). *The Five Giants: A Biography of the Welfare State*. London: Harper Collins.

Townsend, P. (1981). "The structured dependency of the elderly: a creation of social policy in the twentieth century". *Ageing & Society* 1(1): 5–28.

UNICEF Innocenti (2016). "Worlds of influence: understanding what shapes child well-being in rich countries". Innocenti Report Card 16. Florence: UNICEF Office of Research.

Ventola, C. (2015). "The antibiotic resistance crisis. Part I: causes and threats". *Pharmacy and Therapeutics* 40(4): 277–83.

Weaver, M. (2020). "Five already dead by time UK reported first coronavirus death". *The Guardian*, 30 April. https://www.theguardian.com/world/2020/apr/30/five-already-dead-by-time-uk-reported-first-coronavirus-death.

Wilkinson, R. & K. Pickett (2018). *The Inner Level*. London: Penguin.

Wilmslow, C. (1923). *The Evolution and Significance of the Modern Public Health Campaign*. New Haven, CT: Yale University Press.

Wittenburg, R. *et al.* (2019). "Projections of older people living with dementia and costs of dementia care in the United Kingdom, 2019–2040". CPECP Working Paper 5, LSE.

Women's Budget Group (2020). "Creating a caring economy: a call to action". https://wbg.org.uk/wp-content/uploads/2020/09/WBG-Report-v8-ES-1.pdf.

Woods, R. (2003). "Urban–rural mortality differentials: an unresolved debate". *Population and Development Review* 29(1): 29–46.

World Health Organization (1948). *Constitution of the World Health Organization*. Geneva: World Health Organization.

World Health Organization (2018). "Mental health: strengthening our response". https://www.who.int/news-room/fact-sheets/detail/mental-health-strengthening-our-response.

World Health Organization (2021). "Obesity and overweight". https://www.who.int/news-room/fact-sheets/detail/obesity-and-overweight.

Yarnall, A. *et al.* (2017). "New horizons in multimorbidity in older adults". *Age and Ageing* 46: 882–8.

YMCA (2022). "Out of service: a report examining local authority expenditure on youth services in England and Wales". https://www.ymca.org.uk/wp-content/uploads/2020/01/YMCA-Out-of-Service-report.pdf.

Index

150